#66

LEE

TO KILL A MOCKINGBIRD

NOTES

COLES EDITORIAL BOARD

Bound to stay open

Publisher's Note

Otabind (Ota-bind). This book has been bound using the patented Otabind process. You can open this book at any page, gently run your finger down the spine, and the pages will lie flat.

ABOUT COLES NOTES

COLES NOTES have been an indispensible aid to students on five continents since 1948.

COLES NOTES are available for a wide range of individual literary works. Clear, concise explanations and insights are provided along with interesting interpretations and evaluations.

Proper use of COLES NOTES will allow the student to pay greater attention to lectures and spend less time taking notes. This will result in a broader understanding of the work being studied and will free the student for increased participation in discussions.

COLES NOTES are an invaluable aid for review and exam preparation as well as an invitation to explore different interpretive paths.

COLES NOTES are written by experts in their fields. It should be noted that any literary judgement expressed herein is just that — the judgement of one school of thought. Interpretations that diverge from, or totally disagree with any criticism may be equally valid.

COLES NOTES are designed to supplement the text and are not intended as a substitute for reading the text itself. Use of the NOTES will serve not only to clarify the work being studied, but should enhance the reader's enjoyment of the topic.

0-7740-3382-7

© COPYRIGHT 1991 AND PUBLISHED BY
COLES PUBLISHING COMPANY
TORONTO—CANADA
PRINTED IN CANADA

Manufactured by Webcom Limited
Cover finish: Webcom's Exclusive **Duracoat**

CONTENTS

Harper Lee: Life and Works

(Nelle) Harper Lee is a contemporary Southern writer whose reputation was established with her Pulitzer Prize-winning first novel, *To Kill a Mockingbird.*

She was born in Monroeville, Alabama, on April 28, 1926, the youngest of three children of Amasa C. and Frances Finch Lee. Her father was a lawyer, who practised in partnership with her elder sister, Alice F. Lee, in Monroeville.

Harper Lee attended public schools in Monroeville, spent a short period at Huntington College, and then went to the University of Alabama to study law. She spent a year in England at Oxford University, and then returned to Alabama to finish her law studies. She soon left Alabama again—this time for New York City, to become a writer. It was a desire she had nurtured since she was about seven. To support herself, she took a job as reservation clerk for Eastern Air Lines, and then the British Overseas Airway Corporation.

An unknown writer, Miss Lee approached a literary agent with two essays and three short stories. The agent encouraged her to develop one of the stories into a novel. Thereupon, she gave up her airline job and moved into a cold-water apartment with makeshift furniture. About this lean period in Harper Lee's life, a friend remarked that when she was not invited out by friends for dinner, no one asked whether she was eating. It was while she was serving this apprenticeship that her father became ill in Monroeville and so, she divided her time between New York and her hometown, between her book and her ailing father.

In 1957, Miss Lee submitted the book to the J.B. Lippincott Company. She was told that her novel was actually a series of short stories strung together and she was urged to rewrite it.

For the next two-and-one-half years, Harper Lee reworked the story with the help of her editor, Tay Hohoff. Finally, in July, 1960, the novel, *To Kill a Mockingbird,* was published.

In the April 15, 1961 issue of *Vogue* magazine, Miss Lee published her first magazine article, "Love—In Other Words," in which she described her novel as "a love story pure and simple." Thus, at a time when everyone was wondering if good fiction could be written about people who were capable of loving one another and working for cherished ideals, Miss Lee's novel

1

about a heroic lawyer, beloved and respected by his family and friends, was published to critical acclaim and public acceptance.

Harper Lee's family has always lived in the South, and her roots are there. Indeed, her family is related to the Confederate General, Robert E. Lee.

Long after she published her first novel, her father and sister continued to practise law in the home town, Monroeville, where Harper also lives. Since she lives in a small town, the best-selling novelist does not have much privacy. She claims that her neighbors are Southern people, "and if [Southern people] know you are working at home, they think nothing of walking right in for coffee."

Miss Lee describes writing as the most difficult work in the world. Like William Faulkner, she lives in and writes about the territory she knows best—the South. Probably influenced by her liberal father, she is a Republican in a Democratic South. As an integrationist in a segregationist stronghold, she believes that "there's really just one kind of folks. Folks."

Harper Lee affirms belief in "Catholic emancipation and repeal of the Corn Laws." She collects memoirs of nineteenth-century clergymen and among her favorite authors are Jane Austen, Charles Lamb, Thomas Love Peacock and Robert Louis Stevenson, writers who are all noted for the excellence of their prose style. Aside from reading and writing, she maintains an interest in golf, criminology and music. She also finds time to visit her father's office, and remains exceptionally close to this lawyer who, like Atticus Finch, stands for humility, intelligence and diligence in life and work.

As well as *To Kill a Mockingbird,* Miss Lee has published several essays, including the essay in *Vogue,* and one in *McCalls* magazine.

Introduction to *To Kill a Mockingbird*

"A valiant attempt to combine the dominant themes of contemporary Southern fiction—the recollection of childhood among village eccentrics and the spirit-corroding shame of the civilized white Southerner in the treatment of the Negro," wrote Harding Lemay, New York *Herald Tribune* critic. His review appeared July 10, 1960, in the Sunday Book Review Section, newspaper space usually reserved for comments on important books.

Scout Finch, a little girl growing up in a small Southern town, tells the story of her childhood, when she witnessed the trial of a Negro falsely accused of raping a white woman. The Negro's lawyer is Scout Finch's father, Atticus Finch. He defends the Negro vigorously, though he expects to lose the case. As well as being the story of childhood, it is also the story of the prelude to the civil rights struggle of the American Negro.

The theme of idyllic childhood is acted out by three children: Scout Finch, her brother, Jem, and their friend, Dill Harris. The games they invent to play in a sleepy Southern town of the 1930's center around the town's inhabitants, most notably a family with a hermit. In the town, relatives have married relatives for so many generations that almost everyone is related to one another. A schoolteacher from another county is regarded as a foreigner, because she does not know the idiosyncrasies of the local families. The town is an island unto itself. Almost.

The Negro is no longer the slave who supported the large cotton plantations of the deep South. The Civil War of eighty years ago brought defeat to the South, and freedom to the slave, but it left the black man as a symbol of that defeat, turning him into a social outcast, a subjugated and mistreated scapegoat for much of the Southerner's dissatisfaction.

At the time of the novel, Negro mothers were still teaching their children to survive through servility to the white man. "He's white, he's right," a mother would say to her son.

In the 1930's, following the crash of 1929, nearly everyone was poor. The United States was concerned with its internal problems, not with the political ferment going on in Europe. The United States believed it could go its own way and remained uninvolved in European affairs, in the war that was coming. The country was going through a period of isolationism.

3

Not only were Americans not concerned about what was going on in the rest of the world, but many did not even know what was going on in other parts of their own country. Southerners isolated themselves from the North and the West. Nowhere in the country was anyone concerned with civil rights for Negroes. People wanted only to recover from the depression and mind their own business.

The Negroes themselves did not try to ask the whites for anything. Segregation was a fact; Negroes seemed to accept it. If there was discontent, if they wanted their freedom to study and work as they pleased, they did not let white people know about it. To answer back, to be "pushy," to assert oneself as a man was not done by Negroes who wanted to survive. Many Negroes did not think themselves equal.

However, they did feel free to show resentment against the whites for segregation, when white people came into their part of town. If whites did not let Negroes into white social institutions—schools, churches, clubs—then Negroes, in turn, did not fancy white people invading their world either.

When Jem and Scout are taken by their Negro cook, Calpurnia, to a Negro church one Sunday morning, a Negro woman steps out of the crowd to harass Calpurnia for bringing symbols of social slavery into the Negro ghetto. The woman tries to force the unwelcome little children out of the church. She is stopped, however, by Calpurnia and other Negroes, who band together to welcome the children and protect them from the wrath of the hostile woman.

In church, the children have the surprise of seeing a collection taken up for the wife and children of a man wrongly accused of raping a white woman. (This is the man whom the children's father is defending.) In order to obtain the money, the preacher shuts the doors and makes the people sweat in the hot, closed church, beseeching them to help one of their own. This incident, in a small way, shows the conflict faced by Negroes when asked to support a member of their own race in a fight against the white power structure in the South.

So the white children witness the initial waves of discontent among the Negroes, as they attempt to band together. Not yet demanding their rights to equality on a national scale, they are at least helping each other. They are laying the groundwork for the picket lines, freedom marches, sit-ins and the national Negro organizations, like the National Association for the Advancement of Colored People and the Congress of Racial Equality, which will carry on the work of integrating the entire country.

The lone Negro woman who wanted to force the white children out of the church may be a forerunner of the militant and hostile Negroes who have joined pugnacious groups like the Black Muslims, who advocate violence and hate toward white men.

In the novel, Atticus Finch, a lawyer who believes in justice and the courts of the land, finds himself not only defending a client but also fighting for the equality of the Negro. Unless the jury believes that Negroes are equal, the man cannot be acquitted; and the jury cannot believe in the equality of the Negro. In the 1930's, almost no Southerner could. Atticus Finch and his children, Jem and Scout, receive harsh language and abuse from their neighbors and even from their relatives. There are a few exceptions in town: a middle-aged widow who has been a long-time neighbor and the local newspaperman.

The novel is set in a time when the conscience of the South is being pricked to recognize that the Negro is a man, not an animal, and must be free in the true sense of the word. The few Southerners who accept this idea work for it. Other Southerners, who do not accept it, find that they have to fight it. The social bondage of the Negro is no longer a fact accepted by everyone. It is something to question—to fight or to defend. The rights of the Negro are no longer a joke; they are his due. Frightened Southerners make their first attempts to keep the Negro "in his place"—segregated and doing menial work.

Some Southerners, such as the ignorant father of the girl who claims she was raped by a Negro, do not simply fight Negroes with words and threats. The father and others extend their violence to the white liberals. Thus, Atticus Finch's children are attacked by a white man who wants to keep Negroes down.

The novel is written about a South that is being jolted out of its isolationist mentality. Southern Negroes are about to start fighting for their right to vote, to study and to work like men. This is a book, then, about beginnings.

Out of a story told by a little girl in days of almost complete segregation comes the knowledge that the South is not simply a hotbed of ignorance, whose society cannot possibly be updated.

Out of the tale told by a girl brought up in a decent, idealistic family comes the affirmation that a few white men in the South saw the handwriting on the wall and some, like Atticus Finch, refused to be defeated by intimidation.

Many readers and critics feel that the book is autobiographical—that Scout Finch and Harper Lee represent the same person. How much is fiction and how much is fact only the author knows. Certainly it can be said that Maycomb bears a great physical resemblance to Monroeville, the Southern town where Harper Lee grew up. The trees, the weather, the description of the center of town—all are typical of the South.

It is a quiet place, where eccentric characters live unmolested side by side with their neighbors. If one woman drinks, the most she suffers is being gossiped about. Everyone has a quirk; the quirks are accepted. No one, except for people who want to be left alone, is shunned by society. The specific experience is Southern—Sunday visiting, women's clubs, even the food and the ladylike behavior expected of a Southern girl. Matrons still cling to the notion that the most desirable existence for a girl is one of dressing and behaving like a lady and indulging only in ladylike pursuits—tea pouring, embroidering, entertaining other ladies.

The novel is set in the political and social climate of the 1930s. Although not intended as a sociological study, or a judgment of the morality of people in those years, the book is nevertheless socially enlightening and timely. It shows the beginnings of the Negro's fight for equality. It shows the prejudice the Negro was up against, and it shows that Negroes could have some help from decent people like Atticus Finch.

Opposed to this hint of progress in the air, there is a feeling of timelessness, a feeling that nothing has really changed since the Civil War and that most people do not want any change to come about ever. Most people want to stay isolationists, to die proud of their background and family connections, proud of segregating Negroes and resisting their advances.

The feeling that almost no one is going to make a move in favor of progress is backed up by the complete lack of mechanization in the town. There is only one taxi; cars are few. The sky is silent; not a single plane flies overhead during the whole story. Jets are unheard of.

It is only on the ground, in the hands, hearts and minds of a tiny minority, that the first stirrings of progress can be perceived.

Success of the Novel

A great number of critics called *To Kill a Mockingbird* the best novel to appear in a long time. On the other hand, the New York *Herald Tribune* Sunday Book Review declared it was not a book of stature. However, to compare Harper Lee's first novel with the great American novels that have stood the test of time, such as works by Hemingway or Faulkner, is unfair. Harper Lee is new to the literary scene, but her book is technically competent and emotionally winning. Her writing is plain and simple, not tricky or experimental as are many of the books written by her contemporaries. She is both a serious and a popular writer. Many books have been praised by critics and yet have not enjoyed record-breaking waves of popularity, as has Miss Lee's book. While few novelists have become immortals with their first novels, her book shows talent and mastery of craft.

Modern, experimental writers and their fans consider her fiction charming and old-fashioned. She is a writer who employs the scenic method of writing: telling a story scene by scene in rich detail, thus following the traditional form of novelists since the nineteenth century.

Events are told in chronological order, as they happen. Her subject matter and tone of voice are not caught up in any fad. One reviewer thought that her simple, traditional way of telling a story showed that she wrote with one eye on Hollywood. While it is true that her book was adapted easily to the screen, it is to be doubted that the work was primarily oriented toward that medium.

In the year following publication, the book sold more than two-and-one-half million copies, and rode the crest of almost every best-seller list in the country, creating one of the extraordinary records in publishing history. It has now sold well over 12 million copies.

Miss Lee received the literary award of the Alabama Library Association in April, 1961. She also received the Pulitzer Prize for Fiction in May, 1961—the first woman to receive this award since 1942. She was awarded the *Bestseller's* paperback of the year award for 1962, and was honored with the Brotherhood Award of the National Conference of Christians and Jews.

The novel became a Literary Guild selection, a Book-of-the-Month Club alternative and a *Reader's Digest* Condensed Book.

The producer-director team of Robert Mulligan and Alan Pakula acquired film rights and, Gregory Peck, as the hero, Atticus Finch, won Hollywood's Academy Award for Best Actor of the Year.

The book succeeded in London, too, where it was published by William Heinemann, Ltd., and was a British Book Society choice. Rights to it were bought by ten European countries, including France, Germany, Italy and Czechoslovakia.

If it is rare for *any* book to receive such distinction, it is almost unprecedented for a first novel to merit such acclaim. Perhaps it is the extraordinary plea for human dignity—the belief in individual strength—which has proven this work to be such a popular and a critical success.

The Value of the Book

One reviewer said that "what a greenhorn from the North may enjoy most is how quietly and completely he is introduced to ways of seeing and feeling and acting in the Deep South." Therefore, though not a great book, it is sociologically interesting and illuminating. The book's popularity is due to its simple style, the freshness and intelligence of the narrative, the timeliness of the story, the warmth of the main characters and the gripping events of the story itself.

Nearly all the critics agreed that the character portrayal and the description of the locale of a small Southern town were the two finest ingredients in the book. The *Atlantic Monthly* said that the story was "frankly and completely impossible," because it is supposedly narrated by a young girl but is actually written in the prose of a well-educated adult. The *New York Times* and the New York *Herald Tribune*, however, said the book was written in retrospect, by an adult reflecting upon childhood, and accepted the mature voice speaking through the child. One critic felt that incidents surrounding the trial were melodramatic, while another thought all the scenes were of the highest dramatic caliber, with no false sentimentality.

Important critics thought that the story was intended to be read on a high, intellectual plane. In a time of upheaval and change in the social mores of the South, the book is specifically a plea for justice for Negroes. It illuminates clearly the incredible circumstances they have lived in because of white men who are, in matters other than race, often kind and reasonable.

A few critics found two themes in the book at odds. They said that the themes of innocent childhood and the guilt of Southerners in racial matters were never resolved in terms of each other.

Actually, the book's conclusion is that childhood is passing for Jem and Scout, though they will always remember its pleasures and pains. In addition, Southerners will, in the future, work to remove the injustices against the Negroes. The guilt of the past cannot be obliterated. It will always be remembered, but the future can be different, with men willing to work for it.

Plot Summary

The story begins with Scout and her brother Jem considering the causes that led up to Jem's broken arm. They decide it all started with their "being southerners" and with Dill's arrival one particular summer.

Scout was six, Jem nearly ten and Dill almost seven that first summer. The three children played many games but Dill was most interested in studying the Radley place, home of Boo Radley, the town's phantom bogeyman.

Dill leaves in September and Scout for the first time goes to school where she is shamed by the teacher for already knowing how to read and write. She gets into further trouble when she tries to explain Maycomb County ways to the teacher who is from North Alabama. She ends her first morning in school by fighting with Walter Cunningham, the son of a poor farmer. During the school year Scout and Jem begin finding small gifts hidden in a tree at the edge of the Radley yard.

Summer once again brings Dill and a new game for the children; they act out the story of Boo Radley's life. Not content with this game, Jem and Dill decide to coax Boo out of his house by stuffing a note on the end of a fishing pole through his shutters. When this fails, Jem and Dill decide to go right up to the house and peer in a window. While Jem is leaning into the window, a shadow appears and the children flee while a shotgun blasts the night air. Jem gets his pants caught in the fence and takes them off in order to escape. When he returns for them later that night, he finds that someone has mended them.

Winter brings the pleasure of the children's first snowfall and the fear and sadness of a fire that burns down Miss Maudie's house. During the fire Scout and Jem are sent down the block out of danger's way. While they are shivering in the cold night air, someone gently places a blanket around Scout's shoulders, without her noticing. Since all the townsmen were battling the fire, it could only have been Boo who wrapped her up.

At this point the story begins shifting to more serious issues. Scout learns that her father is defending a Negro, Tom Robinson. Most of the townspeople resent Atticus for taking this case so seriously and Scout and Jem face the ridicule of the other children. When cousin Francis calls Atticus a "nigger-lover" who is disgracing the family, Scout cannot contain her anger and she beats him up.

That Christmas, Scout and Jem get the present they most wanted. Atticus gives them each an air rifle and their Uncle Jack teaches them to shoot. Atticus tells them to be careful about what they shoot. "I'd rather you shot at tin cans in the back yard, but I know you'll go after birds. Shoot all the bluejays you want, if you can hit 'em, but remember it's a sin to kill a mockingbird." Scout asks Miss Maudie to explain this and Miss Maudie says that since mockingbirds live only to make beautiful music and do no harm, it is a sin to kill these innocent birds.

Scout and Jem suspect their father is too old to be much good at anything. He wouldn't teach them how to shoot, he wears eyeglasses and he never acts the way their friends' fathers do. Just when their opinion of him is at its lowest, he regains their admiration by showing his courage when confronted by a mad dog. The sheriff asks Atticus to kill the dog because it must be done with one shot and he is afraid he might miss. Atticus reluctantly takes the rifle and kills the mad dog with one perfectly placed shot. Scout and Jem are surprised and proud of their father.

Jem's seemingly endless patience is defeated by Mrs. Dubose's taunting. When she calls Atticus "trash," he retaliates by cutting the tops off her camellia bushes. His punishment is to read to Mrs. Dubose every day after school for a month. When she dies shortly thereafter, he learns she was trying to break herself of a drug addiction and he had helped her do so by keeping her mind off her problem. Atticus tells the children that Mrs. Dubose had shown remarkable courage in breaking her habit even though she knew she would shortly die. He wanted them to know there are other forms of courage besides the obvious physical ones.

One Sunday Atticus is away so Calpurnia takes the children to the Negro church. They get a glimpse of what her life is like and also learn more about Tom Robinson, the man their father is defending. Aunt Alexandra moves into their house to try to give the children, especially Scout, the benefit of her feminine influence. This makes life difficult for the tomboy Scout.

Dill suddenly appears one night after running away from his mother and her new husband. After Atticus consults Dill's Aunt Rachel and his mother, it is decided that Dill can live with Aunt Rachel for all of his summer vacation.

The good and easy times come to an abrupt end when a group of men confront Atticus and tell him it is too dangerous to move Tom Robinson to the Maycomb jail. Nonetheless, he is moved and Atticus chooses to protect Tom himself by sitting in front of the jail. The children follow him there and find him trying to talk a mob out of its wish to lynch Tom Robinson. It is Scout who unknowingly saves the day by addressing one of the men and asking about his son who is her classmate.

The day of the trial the children sneak into the courthouse and sit with Reverend Sykes in the balcony reserved for Negroes. Atticus is able to prove that Mayella Ewell and her father are lying in their testimony against Tom Robinson, yet the all-white jury still brings in a verdict of guilty. Bob Ewell swears to revenge himself upon Atticus Finch who has disgraced him in public by showing his testimony to be false.

Sometime later, Scout assists Aunt Alexandra at one of her church teas and learns of the sympathy these church-going, white women feel for the Negroes in far away places. During the afternoon she also learns that Tom Robinson is dead.

Hallowe'en comes and Scout takes part in a special pageant. She wears a complicated costume of wire mesh and paper that covers her from head to knees. As she and Jem walk home after the gala, they sense someone behind them. There is a fight and Scout is thrown to the ground. When she gets up she sees Jem being carried home by a stranger. The children's savior is none other than Boo Radley.

Heck Tate, the sheriff, arrives in answer to Atticus' phone call. He reports on his findings in the schoolyard. He found a little girl's dress, a piece of muddy cloth and Bob Ewell lying dead on the ground with a knife stuck in him. At first Atticus believes that Jem killed Ewell in self-defence, but he eventually understands that Arthur Radley killed Bob Ewell in order to save the lives of Jem and Scout. Scout appreciates the effort it took Arthur Radley to emerge from his house and commit an act of violence on her behalf. She tells her father that Arthur Radley is really a nice man after all.

Characters in the Novel

Atticus Finch: A lawyer of high principles in the small, South Alabama town of Maycomb, he defends a Negro accused of rape.

Jem Finch: The son of Atticus and his sister's best friend. Jem greatly matures through the course of the novel. His real name is Jeremy.

Scout Finch: The tomboy daughter of Atticus whose real name is Jean Louise. Scout is the narrator of the novel so we see the events through her eyes. Her perception changes as she matures.

Calpurnia: The Negro cook and nanny to the Finch family, she is largely responsible for raising the children.

Miss Rachel: The Finch's next door neighbor and Dill's aunt.

Dill: Jem and Scout's good friend, Dill, or Charles Baker Harris, lives out of state but spends his summers with his aunt, Miss Rachel.

Boo Radley: The mysterious neighbor who captures the children's imagination. Boo, or Mr. Arthur Radley, has remained hidden in his house for many years.

Mr. Radley: Boo's father who locked Boo up many years before and refused to let him out.

Nathan Radley: Boo's older brother who takes his father's place when he dies and continues to keep Boo locked in the house.

Miss Maudie: A good-natured woman with liberal views who becomes the children's particular friend.

Mrs. Dubose: A crotchety old woman who taunts Jem and Scout whenever they pass her house.

Miss Stephanie Crawford: The neighborhood scold and gossip.

Miss Caroline Fisher: Scout's grade one teacher.

Uncle Jack: Atticus' brother who is a welcome Christmas guest.

Aunt Alexandra: Atticus' sister who tries to instil in the children a sense of proper behavior. Aunt Alexandra comes to stay with the Finches during the trial.

Francis: Scout and Jem's cousin who Scout tries to beat up after he insults her father.

Tom Robinson: The Negro accused of attacking Mayella Ewell. Tom is shown to be a hard-working, God-fearing young man.

Helen Robinson: Tom's wife who goes to work for Link Deas.

Bob Ewell: The drunken, irresponsible father of Mayella, it is he who brings charges against Tom Robinson claiming he witnessed the attack on his daughter.

Mayella Ewell: Bob Ewell's eldest daughter who accuses Tom Robinson of attacking her with sexual intent.

Walter Cunningham: An upright and honest farmer who is also a member of the mob which comes to lynch Tom Robinson.

Walter Cunningham Jr.: The son of a poor but honest farmer and one of Scout's classmates, he tries his best at school and is always neat and clean.

Burris Ewell: One of the poor and ignorant Ewells, he is the dirtiest boy Scout has ever seen.

Chuck Little: A poor boy but a born gentleman and one of Scout's classmates.

Cecil Jacobs: One of Scout's classmates who taunts Scout about her father and then scares her and Jem at Hallowe'en.

Heck Tate: The sheriff of Maycomb County and one of Atticus' friends and supporters during the trial of Tom Robinson.

Judge Taylor: The fair-minded judge who appoints Atticus to defend Tom Robinson.

Reverend Sykes: The Negro minister at Cal's church who finds seats for the children during the trial.

Zeebo: Calpurnia's son and the music superintendent at Cal's church.

Mr. B.B. Underwood: The owner and editor of the town's newspaper.

Dolphus Raymond: A white man who lives with a Negro woman.

Mr. Gilmer: The prosecuting attorney at Tom Robinson's trial.

Link Deas: Tom Robinson's employer who stands up for him in court.

Mrs. Merriweather: A "devout" woman who pities the natives in Africa, she also stages the Hallowe'en pageant in which Scout participates.

Mrs. Farrow: A religious woman who comes to Aunt Alexandra's tea.

Chapter by Chapter Summaries and Commentaries

PART ONE • CHAPTER 1

Summary

Scout, the narrator, recalls the various events leading up to her brother Jem's broken arm. Scout thinks it all started with the Ewells but Jem disagrees. He thinks it started with Dill's first visit and the idea of making Boo Radley appear.

Scout then gives a brief history of her family's position in Maycomb up to the present day. She introduces Atticus, her lawyer father, and Calpurnia, their Negro cook.

The summer Scout was almost six and Jem was nearly ten, Dill Harris arrives at his Aunt Rachel's for a holiday. The three become firm friends and spend much of their time thinking about Boo Radley.

Scout tells the story of Boo who was locked up as a teenager for once getting in trouble with the police. Boo has been in the house ever since, although some people are convinced he comes out at night.

Dill challenges Jem to rup up and touch the Radley house. When Jem does so, the children think they see an inside shutter move.

Commentary

As the novel opens we are aware of two things: Scout, the narrator, is one of the story's main characters, and she is telling the story some years after the events have occurred. The events will all be seen through a young girl's eyes and her emotional development is central to the novel. In fact, each episode contributes to Scout's eventual understanding.

As the novel opens, an air of expectancy is created. We know something has happened to Jem but we don't know what caused it. The Radley place and its mysterious inhabitant are described in great detail and we suspect it will play an important role in the story. The chapter ends with the suspected movement in the house and the tension associated with the house is confirmed.

This opening chapter also serves to pinpoint the locale of the action. Maycomb's inhabitants are described and we learn of the slow, uneventful lives they lead. The later juxtaposition of peaceful, small-town life and violent racism is set up in this chapter. We also learn a little about Atticus, the Finch who broke family tradition by leaving the cotton plantation to study law. His independent nature is necessary when he has to face the town's opposition to his defence of a Negro, Tom Robinson. Scout thinks her father is merely "satisfactory." In this opening chapter we sense his respect for his children in his "courteous detachment." Later, we realize that he is an exceptional father and Jem and Scout's relationship with him, although not an average father-child one, is a close and precious relationship.

Something should also be said of Miss Lee's approach to her material. Miss Lee has made Scout an astute and perceptive narrator with a keen sense of humor. Some of the humor lies in hearing a young girl speak as she does and some arises from her own comic sense. In any case, the humor is a vital part of the novel as it serves to modify the seriousness of many of the events.

Notes

amble – to walk in a leisurely fashion

nebulous – indistinct

repertoire – collection of plays, songs, etc., with which a performer is familiar

vapid – not interesting

transition – a change

mockingbird – American bird of the thrush family which mocks other birds' songs and other sounds

Charles Lamb – English writer, poet and critic (1775-1834)

Andrew Jackson – seventh President of the United States (1829-37)

Atticus – Roman who fled to Greece, resolving to keep detached from politics

Mobile – chief port of Alabama, on the Gulf of Mexico

John Wesley – founder of Wesleyan Methodism

Montgomery – State capital of Alabama

collard – variety of cabbage

chinaberry trees – azaderac, tall tree; also known as bead-tree

johnson grass — tropical grass similar to Indian corn

Auburn – town 125 miles north-east of Monroeville

Pensacola – city and port of Florida

cannas – tropical plant

CHAPTER 2

Summary

Scout starts school that September and learns that "school's different" from anything she has known. She has problems from the beginning. Miss Caroline, Scout's teacher, is upset to learn that Scout already reads and makes her promise to do no more reading with her father. When she finds Scout writing a letter to Dill she again reprimands her, saying "in the first grade they will learn to print and writing will not be taught until the third grade."

Scout's third confrontation with Miss Caroline takes place when she tries to explain the ways of the Cunninghams, a family of poor but proud farmers who refuse charity. Miss Caroline thinks Scout is being insolent and after slapping her hand, sends Scout into the corner.

Commentary

Here we see Scout's formal education in action. The school system is mocked for working so hard at limiting a student's education. Scout is chastised for knowing how to read and told to forget what she already knows and begin again with the basics. Shortly afterward it emerges that she also knows how to write, a skill that will have to be put aside until grade three when she can learn it all over again. Miss Lee has written this chapter with a gentle sense of humor while also suggesting that school is not where Scout's major lessons are learned.

One incident to be noted in this chapter is the introduction of Walter Cunningham, a poor farmboy who nevertheless made the effort to attend school in a "clean shirt and neatly mended overalls." The Cunningham family is described as "proud and respectable folks who have been hit hard by the depression." They reject charity, taking only what they can pay for. Walter Cunningham's father is a member of the lynch mob that later comes for Tom Robinson. The mob is stopped when Scout addresses Mr. Cunningham and asks about his entailment and sends her hello to his son.

Notes
illicitly – unlawfully
vexations – annoyances

mortification – humiliation
catawba – American grape
scrip stamp – charity tokens to be exchanged for goods
smilax – decorative plant
WPA – Works Progress Administration, introduced by F. D.
  Roosevelt

CHAPTER 3

Summary

In a continuation of earlier events, Scout beats up Walter Cunningham for getting her off on the wrong foot at school. Jem makes her stop and then invites Walter home for lunch. Atticus treats their guest politely, speaking to him of farm matters. When Scout interrupts to comment on Walter's manners, she is made to leave the table and lectured furiously by Calpurnia. A guest, she is told, is to be treated with respect, no matter what he does.

In school that afternoon another of the town's poor families is introduced. Burris Ewell has lice and is the filthiest person Scout has ever seen. Unlike Walter Cunningham, Burris makes no attempt at dressing for school and has no intention of returning to the classroom after the first day.

Scout's first day of school was a hard one and she begs Atticus to let her stay home thereafter. Atticus tells Scout that she has learned a lot today and that if she tries to see things from another's point of view, she will get along just fine.

Atticus goes on to explain why Scout has to go to school and Burris Ewell doesn't. The Ewells are not like regular folks, he says. Their disgraceful behavior and the fact they live like animals places them outside the norm of civilized people.

Commentary

Scout's major lessons today came from Calpurnia, who taught her that a guest is deserving of respect no matter who he is, and from Atticus, who tries to impart the important message that to better understand a person we should try to see things through their eyes. These words echo throughout the book and in the end Scout successfully imagines Boo's vision of life.

We also learn of the Ewell's particular place outside

society's jurisdiction which prepares us for Mr. Ewell's vengeful attack on the children. The contrast between the poor and respectable Cunninghams and the disreputable Ewells assumes greater importance during the trial.

It is also briefly mentioned that Scout passed the Radley house four times that day, "twice at a full gallop." In this way Miss Lee keeps the Radley mystery in our minds.

Notes
iniquities – sins, wrongdoings, injustices
fractious – unruly, irritable
hain't – ghost

CHAPTER 4

Summary
Scout describes the endless boredom of the first grade which is relieved only when she finds something hidden in one of the oak trees at the edge of the Radley property. When she investigates, she finds two pieces of gum. On the last day of school she finds another treasure: two gift-wrapped Indian-head pennies.

Dill arrives for the summer holidays and the children play a game called Boo Radley. The game involves acting out the story of Boo's life. Scout tires of the game and is relieved when Atticus appears and makes them stop. She also reveals that when she once rolled in a tire into the Radley yard, she thought she heard someone within the house laughing quietly.

Commentary
The opening section of this chapter further indicates the little use Scout has for her formal education. The school system seems determined to keep her as bored as possible for as long as possible.

The only event of interest in Scout's school year is the finding of two gifts in the Radley tree. We suspect, although Scout doesn't, that the gifts come from Boo. It seems unlikely he is the monster imagined by Scout and Jem if he leaves gifts for the children in the tree. The sense of mystery about the house and its inhabitant is furthered when Scout thinks she hears laughter coming from within the house after she falls out of a tire on the Radley's front lawn.

Boo is an example of the unknown to the children and they endlessly act out the "melancholy little drama" of his life. To Atticus, Boo Radley is a human being and he orders the children to stop their game.

Notes
Indian heads – old American one-cent pieces
scuppernong – variety of American grape

CHAPTER 5

Summary
Jem and Dill spend more time together, to the exclusion of Scout, so she develops a warm friendship with Miss Maudie. Miss Maudie loves the outdoors and spends all of her time there. She also loves everything in "God's earth" except nut grass. She is the children's friend because she keeps their secrets. One evening Scout asks Miss Maudie about Boo Radley. Miss Maudie tells her his name is Mr. Arthur and he is just a man who has chosen to remain in his house. We see in Miss Maudie the same respect for others that exists in Atticus.

Jem and Dill come up with a plan to make Boo emerge. They decide to pass him a note on the end of a fishing pole. Atticus catches them in the act and lectures them on Mr. Radley's right to privacy. If he wants to come out he will do so, and if he chooses not to, that is his right, Atticus tells them.

Commentary
Miss Maudie's warmth and respect for the children is the basis of their friendship. Her open-mindedness and sense of justice is seen here in connection with the Radleys. She feels Arthur's privacy should be respected. He is, after all, a human being and not a phantom. Her attitudes assume greater importance later during the difficult days of the trial when Miss Maudie supports Atticus' decision. Miss Maudie also discounts the gossipy Miss Stephanie's story of seeing Boo peeking through her window. She asked Miss Stephanie if she moved over in the bed. It is interesting to note that Scout assumes Miss

Stephanie shut up because of Miss Maudie's loud voice while we readers realize it was the sexual innuendo that silenced Miss Stephanie.

Notes
nut grass – variety of American grass
Nashville – capital of Tennessee
Second Battle of the Marne – First World War offensive of allies
   against the Germans

CHAPTER 6

Summary
Jem and Dill are determined to have one last attempt at seeing Boo Radley. They have decided on the last night of summer to peek in through the broken shutter. Scout protests, but goes along with the plan. Jem is on the back porch peering in a window when the shadow of a man appears. The man approaches Jem, reaches out with one hand then turns back in the direction he came from. The children race through the Radley backyard and under the fence. As they run a shot is fired at them. Jem's pants get caught in the fence and he takes them off in order to escape.

Feigning nonchalance the children join the circle of adults outside the Radley house. Nathan Radley tells how he shot at a Negro in his collard patch. Of course they all notice that Jem is without his pants and Dill quickly explains they were playing strip poker. Later that night Jem goes back to the Radley place for his pants.

Commentary
The Radley place has again been central to the children's summer plans and this final attack on the mysterious house marks the end of the second summer. The children have approached the darkened house and meet a man on the porch. He stretches out an arm and then retreats. It seems likely this was the mysterious Boo Radley, who later in the novel stretches out his hand to touch Jem's hair.

Notice how visual the description in this and other chapters is, and imagine these scenes in a movie. Too, it becomes obvious that Boo's relationship with the children is central to the story and has been carefully constructed from the start.

Notes
kudzu – ornamental plant from the Orient

CHAPTER 7

Summary
It takes Jem a week to tell Scout that his pants had been mended and were neatly folded on the fence the night he went back for them.

When school starts the oak tree again begins yielding small gifts: a ball of twine, soap carvings of Jem and Scout, gum, a spelling medal and, best of all, a pocket watch. The children write the gift-giver a thank you note, intending to put it into the tree. When they arrive at the tree the next day, they find the hole plugged up with cement.

It takes a couple of days until the children can stop Mr. Nathan Radley and ask him why he stopped up the knothole. He tells them the tree was dying and he was trying to save it. When Jem consults Atticus, Atticus says the tree seems healthy. Jem sits outside and silently cries.

Commentary
Scout, not realizing the real reason for Jem's moodiness, nevertheless follows Atticus' advice and tries to review that night's events through Jem's eyes. For her patience and understanding she earns Jem's confidence and he tells her about his mended pants.

As the children continue finding gifts in the tree we see that Jem begins to suspect Boo is their secret friend. Scout, however, has no inkling of this. In a clever manner, Miss Lee has Scout describing Jem's dawning awareness, while Scout herself remains ignorant.

When the children try to thank their friend in a letter, Mr. Nathan stops them from doing so by cementing the hole. Jem realizes that Mr. Nathan is preventing his brother Boo from pursuing the friendship and it is this realization that makes Jem weep.

Notes
camel-kicked – kicked sideways, surreptitiously

CHAPTER 8

Summary

That winter is an unusual one for the children. They see their first snowfall, and although there is only a few inches of snow on the ground they decide to make a snowman. By bringing snow from their backyard and using a base of mud, they make a reasonable snowman. Jem's artistic talent comes to the fore as the snowman assumes an unmistakable resemblance to their neighbor, Mr. Avery.

As the temperature drops that night, every fireplace in the house is kept going. Scout is awakened by her father shortly after one o'clock and told to get dressed. Then she and Jem are sent down the street to stand outside the Radley's gate. Miss Maudie's house is burning and there is fear that the Finch's house will also catch fire. Scout stands shivering in the cold as the men battle to put the fire out. When the children return to their house after the fire has been doused, Atticus points to a blanket around Scout's shoulders and asks where it came from. As neither Scout nor Jem seems to know how it got around her shoulders, Jem and Atticus conclude it was placed there by Boo Radley. Scout is scared silly when they tell her who gave her the blanket.

The next morning Miss Maudie is already hard at work trying to clean up her garden. She accepts good-naturedly the catastrophe which befell her.

Commentary

In this chapter it becomes clear that Boo Radley wants to be friends with the children. Now even Scout seems to recognize that he is not the fearsome creature the children had first imagined. Jem realizes more fully than Scout the nature of their friend and cannot help himself from telling Atticus all the secrets of their relationship.

With this important fact established, the role of Boo Radley fades for the time being and the story shifts to the events surrounding the trial of Tom Robinson.

Notes

unfathomable – impossible to understand
aberration – departure from what is usual or correct
Rosetta Stone – tablet of black rock discovered in the Nile delta,
     erected in honor of a king
Appomattox – General Lee surrendered to General Grant in
     Virginia in a small town called Appomattox
Bellingraths – gardens in Theodore, near Mobile

CHAPTER 9

Summary

One day at school Scout gets into a fight with a boy who says that her daddy defends "niggers." When Scout asks Atticus about the truth of this claim, he replies that he is defending a Negro, Tom Robinson, and that most of the town feels he shouldn't take the case. He tells her to expect to hear some rather nasty talk about the affair from her classmates and he asks her to "hold her head high and to keep her fists down."

Atticus tries to explain to Scout the reasons for taking on a battle when one knows ahead of time there is no chance of winning the fight. She is not sure that she understands but does realize that to get into a fist fight would be to let Atticus down. She sticks to her resolve until that Christmas when her cousin Francis gets the better of her when he calls Atticus a "nigger-lover" and a disgrace to the family. Scout beats him up and is severely dealt with by her Uncle Jack.

Later that evening Scout teaches Uncle Jack how little he knows about children saying that her father would never judge a situation by hearing only one side of a story.

Jem and Scout are given air rifles for Christmas and Uncle Jack teaches them to shoot.

Commentary

Life is becoming more complicated for Scout as the day of the trial draws near. Her friends at school have begun teasing her and she is warned by Atticus that the taunting and name calling will get even worse.

Christmas is celebrated at Aunt Alexandra's and becomes the occasion for several important lessons. Uncle Jack spanks

24

Scout without having heard her side of the story. She later teaches him that this is not the way Atticus would have handled the situation. Atticus is reasonable and rational and knows that every issue has two sides to it. Uncle Jack learns this but makes another mistake. When Scout asks him the meaning of the word "whore-lady" he changes the subject without answering the question. This time Atticus tells him that he handled the situation wrongly. Children's questions should always be answered. In this chapter we are seeing Atticus' nature emerge more clearly. He is the voice of calm and understanding in the midst of the storm.

Atticus' principles are such that he feels obliged to defend Tom Robinson in spite of the town's opposition. When explaining the case to Scout he doesn't tell her that he had no choice in taking on the case. Instead, he tries to teach her the meaning of morality and courage. He has taken this case because he believes in the issues at stake. He will fight his hardest to win the case, even though he is bound to lose, because that is the true meaning of moral courage.

Although Atticus is sure of the rightness of his actions he worries about Scout's reaction to some of the ugly things she will hear. He tries to tell her it is better to fight with one's head than with one's fists and uses the night-time conversation with Uncle Jack to emphasize his point. Atticus realizes that Scout is standing in the hallway and listening in on their conversation. Thus, he turns the conversation to his major concern; whether or not Scout will be able to tolerate without anger the nasty words she is bound to hear. By allowing Scout to overhear this conversation, Atticus is ensuring the effect his words will have. We later see the outcome of reacting with one's fists instead of with calm, measured thought when the lynch mob comes to take Tom Robinson.

The Tom Robinson case is the second plot of the book. For the moment Boo Radley is all but forgotten as this second story unfolds. Later the two plots come together when Boo saves the children's lives.

It is possible to see both Boo Radley and Tom Robinson as examples of the harmless mockingbird, but more importantly they both serve indirectly as Scout's teachers. The lessons they impart are about respect, morality and courage.

Notes
provocation – something or someone who disturbs another
umbrage – offense
oppressive – burdensome
still – apparatus for distilling liquor; stills are illegal
Confederate veteran – one who was a soldier in the army of the
    Confederate States (the South) in the American Civil War
General Hood – a Confederate general (1831-1879)
Missouri Compromise – consists of several legal bills of the U.S.
    Congress which were necessary to enact before Missouri
    could be admitted as the twenty-fourth state in 1820
Stonewall Jackson – nickname for Thomas Jonathan Jackson,
    a general of the Confederate army; also known as **Ol' Blue-
    light**
Rose Aylmer – a cat named after the main character of a poem
    by W. S. Laudor
catwalk – narrow ledge
widow's walk – observation platform
Lord Melbourne – an English Prime Minister

CHAPTER 10

Summary

The children begin to suspect their father is too old to be good at anything. He certainly doesn't behave the way most of their friends' fathers do. He doesn't even teach the children how to shoot with their air rifles, leaving that task to their Uncle Jack. He does tell them, however, that they must never shoot at mockingbirds. To do so is a sin.

Scout asks Miss Maudie about this and learns that mockingbirds are harmless creatures who live only to make beautiful music and therefore should be allowed to live in peace.

One day the children see a dog behaving in a strange fashion and tell Calpurnia. She recognizes that the dog is rabid and calls Atticus. When Atticus and Heck Tate, the sheriff, arrive, Mr. Tate asks Atticus to shoot the dog. It is a one shot job and Mr. Tate feels that he is not a good enough shot to do it. To the children's surprise, Atticus takes the rifle and shoots the dog with one shot. Miss Maudie later tells them that Atticus "was the deadest shot in Maycomb County" and used to be known as "Ol' One-Shot." Jem realizes that his father has not told them about this talent because he is basically a peace-loving man and because a gentleman doesn't brag about his accomplishments.

Commentary

In this chapter we come across the reason for the title of the novel. Killing mockingbirds is a sin, the only sin that Scout has ever heard Atticus mention. The reason, as already stated, is that these birds sing their hearts out for us while doing absolutely no harm.

Scout and Jem are beginning to notice that their father is different from the other fathers they know and first they think this means he is not as good as they are. Atticus dispels this notion by demonstrating both his physical courage and his skill when he shoots the rabid dog. This is a form of courage that Scout can accept more easily than the moral courage it takes to defend Tom Robinson. Although Jem understands why Atticus has never bragged about this talent to his children, Scout thinks he has just forgotten to mention it. She still doesn't understand her father.

Notes
corncribs – mangers, fodder-racks
mausoleum – tomb

CHAPTER 11

Summary

The children have always regarded Mrs. Dubose as the terror of the neighborhood and avoided passing her house. Jem now decides that he is old enough to encounter anything she can offer. Unfortunately he has underestimated Mrs. Dubose in more than one way. She manages to make him lose his temper by saying his father is "no better than the niggers and trash he works for." To retaliate, Jem cuts the tops off all her camellia bushes. When he goes to apologize, Mrs. Dubose sets his punishment at reading to her every day after school for a month.

Scout goes with Jem to read to Mrs. Dubose. The first day

they read to her for twenty minutes before they are sent away. They go every day, staying longer and longer each day. After the month plus one week is over the children forget all about Mrs. Dubose until one day she dies. Atticus explains that she had been a morphine addict who had wanted to break her addiction before she died. Jem's reading to her had been a little distraction to take her mind off the agony she was going through. Atticus also points out the courage Mrs. Dubose had, to want to die free of her addiction.

Commentary

The primary object of this chapter is to teach the children about another form of courage. Chapter 10 shows the children impressed with Atticus' marksmanship. He wants them to realize that courage is not a "man with a gun in his hand. It's when you known you're licked before you begin but you begin anyway and you see it through no matter what." This is the courage that Mrs. Dubose possessed in order to beat her addiction, and it is also the courage of Atticus who chooses to defend Tom Robinson while knowing from the start he can never win.

Notes
C.S.A. - Confederate States of America
mutts - fools, blockheads

PART TWO • CHAPTER 12

Summary

One Sunday when Atticus is away on business, Calpurnia takes Jem and Scout to the Negro church she attends rather than leaving them alone in their own church. One woman, Lula, protests at permitting white children into their church but the children are made to feel welcome by the Reverend Sykes who proclaims from the pulpit that they are more than welcome because of their father. After the service he tells the children that the church has no better friend than their father.

Scout is interested in how the service will be run since there are no hymn books. Calpurnia tells her it wouldn't do much good if there were hymn books since very few of the Negroes can read. Instead they sing the hymns one line at a time as Zeebo, Calpurnia's son, leads the congregation. *Lining*, as this method of singing is called, is the way the hymns have been sung for as long as Calpurnia can remember. Before the service is over the Reverend Sykes takes up a collection for Helen Robinson, Tom's wife. He doesn't allow anyone to leave the church until the collection reaches ten dollars.

Commentary

In Part II, the plot becomes more focused on the events surrounding Tom Robinson's trial. The division of the novel into two parts emphasizes the difference between the relatively carefree days before the trial and the sudden loss of innocence that the trial forces upon Scout, Jem and Dill.

In Part II all the children's assumptions about life are destroyed. In Chapter 12 we see how surprised they are with evidence of Calpurnia's separate life. They are also taken aback to realize their presence at the church is resented by one of the Negro women. In the following chapters, Scout is often surprised at the behavior of her father; unpleasantly so when he tries to subscribe to Aunt Alexandra's values, and with fear and pride when she realizes he faced the lynch mob with only a newspaper in his lap. The trial's outcome shocks and saddens the children, especially Jem who loses his faith in the goodness of mankind. In yet another surprising episode, Scout sees her Aunt Alexandra break down and cry and comes to realize that there is more to being a lady than she thought there was. The final assumption to be destroyed is the one about the monster Boo Radley. When Scout sees him as he really is, a quiet and timid man, the last of her illusions collapses, and she is well on the road to maturity.

Chapter 12 opens with a scene from the life of Maycomb's Negro population. The children are surprised to see how openly their presence is resented by Lula, although Reverend Sykes warmly welcomes them. During the trial we will see how he takes special care of the children when most of the other adults are too preoccupied to care about them. The children are beginning to learn that each individual must be judged by his own worth and not by the color of his skin. Just as the Ewells, who are white, are lazy and untrustworthy, so Lula, who is black, is bad-tempered and unfriendly.

For the first time the children realize that Calpurnia has another life when she is not working for them. They are interested in the circumstances of her upbringing and learn that she has been connected with their family for a very long time. This segment reveals the chasm that exists between the white and black communities in Maycomb. It also brings to the children's attention the personal circumstances of Tom Robinson and his family, making his trial all the more meaningful to them.

Notes

Birmingham – Birmingham, Alabama — an important industrial town of Jefferson County, about 140 miles north of Monroeville.

Shadrach – Shadrach, Meschach and Abed-nego were three Jews whom Nebuchadnezzar, the King of Babylon, ordered to be cast into "a burning fiery furnace" as a punishment for refusing to worship a golden image. (See the Book of Daniel, Ch. 3.)

Octagon soap – the brand name of a kind of laundry soap

castile – soap, made with olive-oil and soda

Mardi Gras – the last day of the Lenten carnival, celebrated with all sorts of festivities on Shrove Tuesday

asafoetida – a resinous gum with a strong smell of garlic

Hunt – William Holman Hunt, an English painter (1827-1910)

Blackstone's Commentaries — the main textbook of English law at one time.

CHAPTER 13

Summary

The children come home from church to find Aunt Alexandra moving into their house for a visit of indeterminate length. She and Atticus have decided that her presence will be necessary during the difficult summer ahead, and Aunt Alexandra has decided the children, especially Scout, are at an age when they need a little feminine influence. Maycomb makes Aunt Alexandra welcome by inviting her to join all of its leading organizations.

Aunt Alexandra's major preoccupation is with heredity and the family's position in Maycomb. She tries to impress upon the children the importance of their position in the town. When she fails to make her ideas clear, she enlists Atticus' aid. He tries to speak to the children but he is uncomfortable with the subject and finally tells the children to forget what he has said and to go on acting the way they always have.

Commentary

Whatever ill we think of Aunt Alexandra we should recognize that she has come to help Atticus in the difficult days ahead even though she doesn't agree with his views. When she tries to impress upon the family a sense of its own importance, she puts Atticus in an awkward position. He doesn't want to contradict his sister but he feels an individual should be judged on his own worth and not by his family name. He tries to tell the children what Aunt Alexandra wants but ends by telling the children to forget what he has just said. He realizes that his relationship with them is not worth risking by teaching something he does not believe in.

Notes

Rice Christians – people who convert to Christianity for material benefit

Creek Nation – group of Indian tribes who occupied the area north of Florida

CHAPTER 14

Summary

Aunt Alexandra's influence is not felt again for some time.

But when Scout recounts the events of the Sunday they went to church with Cal, Aunt Alexandra is so upset she tells Atticus he should dismiss Cal. He says Cal is part of the family and will never leave.

That night Scout gets into a fight with her brother after he tells her not to antagonize their aunt. Scout, resenting Jem's telling her what to do, attacks him. Both children are sent to bed.

As Scout is getting into her bed, she steps on something she believes to be a snake. She calls Jem for help. The snake under the bed turns out to be Dill who has run away from home. In a terrible betrayal of the children's unity, Jem tells Atticus that Dill is hiding in their bedroom. Atticus talks the matter over with Dill's Aunt Rachel and his mother, and Dill is permitted to stay the night.

Commentary

In this chapter we see Scout's confusion as Atticus seems to change before her eyes. In the first place he argues with his sister about Cal and he tries to get the children to understand the importance of their family position, a concept he himself ignores. These changes are the result of the tension he is experiencing because of Tom Robinson's trial. Scout doesn't understand this although Jem does.

CHAPTER 15

Summary

Dill is permitted to stay for the summer with his Aunt Rachel. Within the week, however, the carefree days of summer turn into a nightmare.

One night a group of men come to speak with Atticus about the danger of transferring Tom Robinson to the Maycomb jail. To Jem, their mood seems ominous. When the men move a few steps closer to Atticus, Jem, who is watching from the darkened livingroom window with the other children, calls out to Atticus that the phone is ringing. Atticus tells him to answer it and the men dissolve into laughter. Scout notes that they were men they saw every day, neighbors and friends. Atticus explains to Jem that these men were their friends and that he didn't have to fear mobs in Maycomb.

Scout returns from walking Dill home and overhears Atticus and Aunt Alexandra arguing in the livingroom. Aunt Alexandra is against Atticus defending Tom Robinson. When Scout confronts Jem, he tells her he is worried about Atticus. He is afraid someone will hurt him. Scout doesn't understand why and thinks that Jem is just being mysterious.

The next night Jem sees Atticus leave the house and decides to follow him. Scout and Dill go with him. The children find Atticus sitting on a chair outside the jail reading a newspaper. As they watch, a crowd of men approach Atticus and ask him to give them Tom Robinson. Scout, thinking it would be a fine surprise for her father, runs through the crowd and straight to him. Jem and Dill follow. Atticus orders Jem to take the children home but Jem refuses to listen. Scout searches through the crowd for a familiar face and sees Mr. Cunningham. She calls hello to him and tries to involve him in a conversation, first by asking about his entailment, a legal problem which Atticus had helped him with, and then by sending her greetings to his son, Walter. Mr. Cunningham at first refuses to respond. When he finally does, the tension dissipates and the men all go home. After they have left, Mr. Underwood, the newspaper editor, tells Atticus that he had him covered with his shotgun all the time.

Commentary

In this chapter we see the results of reacting without thinking. This mob wants violence and Atticus stands alone against it. His courage is expressed through his calm words and manner. He carries no weapon but counts on the innate good sense in every man to realize the wrongness of their position. Scout doesn't realize what is happening and therefore doesn't see that her father is in any danger. She reacts with the naturalness of a child and when she spies a familiar face in the mob, she is quick to greet him.

When Walter Cunningham finally acknowledges Scout's greeting he realizes the wrongness of the mob. He recognizes Atticus as a man and not just a roadblock, as a father like himself and as the man who helped him with his legal difficulties. When Scout sends greetings to his son he also realizes the basic decency that is in Atticus and his children. Acknowledging all of this, he disperses the crowd.

Using Scout as the narrator allows Miss Lee to present things through her eyes without the understanding the reader has of the situation. In this way the events have both an added dimension and an added tension.

Mr. Underwood's emergence at the end of the chapter with the news that he had Atticus covered with his shotgun all the time is interesting. Mr. Underwood dislikes Negroes but is shown to believe, nevertheless, in the right of each man to a legal trial. This gives us the idea that the law is important no matter what a man's race. As we see, however, the law can still ignore the facts and convict a man just because of his color.

Notes
Henry W. Grady – famous journalist and editor whose speeches helped reconcile animosities after the Civil War
Gothic – style of architecture
Jitney Jungle – entertainment arcade (jitney is U.S. slang for "nickel")

CHAPTER 16

Summary
The next day, the day of the trial, Scout asks Atticus about Mr. Cunningham's friendship. She had thought he was their friend. Atticus replies that he is a friend who became part of a mob and forgot he was an individual until Scout called attention to him.

As Atticus is leaving for the courthouse, he tells the children to stay away from the downtown area that day. Jem, Dill and Scout sit on the front porch and watch the people passing by on their way to the trial. Jem describes the local characters to Dill. When Mr. Dolphus Raymond passes by, Dill is surprised to see him drinking from a brown paper bag. Jem explains he keeps whiskey in a bottle inside the bag so as not to offend the ladies. The children decide to go to the courthouse but when they arrive they are unable to find any seats. Reverend Sykes makes room for them in the balcony reserved for the Negroes. When the children are seated they see that Judge Taylor is on the bench and Mr. Heck Tate is in the witness box.

Commentary

Although Scout is not aware of the state of Atticus' nerves, we sense he is feeling the strain when he refuses his breakfast. Then too, he is a little short with Aunt Alexandra when he tells her Calpurnia has the right to speak about anything she chooses. He doesn't lose his temper, however. He is always calm and rational.

Atticus explains to Scout that although a mob sometimes seems to act of its own accord, it really is made up of individuals. If you can make the members of a mob realize that they still have personal choices, you can destroy it. When Scout called attention to Mr. Cunningham she reminded him that he was a man and a father and she made him stand in Atticus' shoes for a moment. As soon as he did this he could see the wrongness of his actions. Here we see the original lesson repeated again.

Miss Maudie, whom we have seen to be a sensible and well-respected individual, offers the opinion that the townspeople have turned the trial into a morbid ''Roman carnival'' and she refuses to participate in such an event. Miss Maudie is a barometer of decency in the novel. She also understands that there is very little hope of Tom Robinson winning his case and therefore sees the morbidity of watching him condemned to certain death.

Mr. Dolphus Raymond's story is included to offer a contrast to Atticus. Mr. Raymond prefers the company of Negroes to that of whites but doesn't have the courage to stand by his feelings. Instead he presents himself as a drunkard so that Maycomb will have an excuse for his behavior.

On their way into the courthouse, Scout learns that her father was appointed to defend Tom Robinson. She wonders why people are so upset with Atticus since they all know he was appointed to the job. What Scout doesn't know, but the reader does, is that the town wishes Atticus to perform only the most perfunctory job. They don't want him to tell the truth and they don't want him to put up a good defence. In their minds, Atticus should believe Tom Robinson guilty and should wish to see him hanged just as they do.

When the children accept Reverend Sykes' offer of a seat in the Negro section, we see what true lack of prejudice is. The children have not been taught the racial prejudice which taints most of the townspeople, so they see nothing wrong in sitting where there is an available seat.

Notes
Braxton Bragg – a brave but unsuccessful Confederate general
Mennonites – members of a Protestant sect similar in beliefs to
      Quakers and Baptists (named for founder, Menno Simons
      (1492-1559)
William Jennings Bryan – Americal politician (1860-1925)
      famous as a public speaker

CHAPTER 17

Summary

Heck Tate testifies that he was called by Bob Ewell to arrest
Tom Robinson because he had raped his daughter. Mayella
Ewell was bruised and beaten and had a blackened right eye.

Bob Ewell testifies he heard his daughter scream and then
saw Tom Robinson run away from the house. Scout reports that
there was an uproar in the courtroom during Bob Ewell's testimony and the Reverend Sykes wants Jem to take her and Dill
home but Jem refuses to leave. Before he is through testifying,
Ewell confirms Heck Tate's analysis of the events and says
Mayella's injuries were primarily to the right side of her face.
Atticus asks Ewell whether he can read and write and asks him
to write his name on a piece of paper. Mr. Ewell writes his name
with his left hand and Scout reasons that her father is trying to
show that a left-handed person causes injuries to the right side
of the face when he punches. Scout worries, however, that Tom
Robinson may also prove to be left-handed.

Commentary

In this chapter we learn something about the Ewell's living
conditions. They live in great squalor behind the town garbage
dump. There are no windows in their shack, only holes in the
walls. The children play with anything they find in the dump
that isn't worth eating. Nobody even knows how many children
lived in the shack with their father; some say six, others say
nine. We learn more about their life in the following chapter
when Atticus questions Mayella Ewell.

In questioning Heck Tate and Bob Ewell, Atticus has raised
two important points for the jury's consideration. He first
established that the injuries were all on the right side of

Mayella's face, leading one to assume that a left-handed person had beat her, and secondly he questioned why no one had sent for a doctor to examine Mayella if her injuries were so severe and, most particularly, if she had been raped.

Notes
frog-sticking without a light – not having taken sufficient precautions

CHAPTER 18

Summary
Mayella Ewell is called to the stand and tries to win the court's sympathy by crying. As Atticus questions her about the circumstances of her life, we learn that she is 19 years old, the eldest of seven children and that there is never enough to eat nor shoes to wear when the weather is cold.

Atticus questions her about her relationship with Tom Robinson and she replies that he had never been inside the fence before. When Atticus asks her to identify the man who raped her, she points to Tom Robinson. When Tom Robinson stands up the children see that his left arm is twelve inches shorter than his right arm and that his left hand is completely useless.

Commentary
Mayella's life is slowly brought to light by Atticus' questions. We learn of the hardship that goes on in the shack behind the dump; the relief cheque that is spent on booze by their father; the tires they cut up to wear as shoes in the winter; the water they haul from a stream at the other side of the dump. We also learn a little of Mayella's loneliness. When Atticus asks whether she has any friends, Mayella thinks he is making fun of her.

Through his skilful questioning, Atticus shows that Mayella's story cannot be true. Tom Robinson's injured arm makes it unlikely he could have choked and beaten a strong girl who was fighting him off. From the questions Mayella refuses to answer we get an idea of what might really have happened. It seems likely Mayella was beaten by her father and that this was not the first time it had happened. She starts to say her father is

37

tolerable when he hasn't been drinking, but doesn't finish the sentence. When Atticus asks her whether her father ever goes after her, she pauses and gazes around the courtroom before replying that her father had "never touched a hair o' my head."

Since Atticus has shown both Mayella and her father to be liars, their anger and hatred for him knows no bounds. It is this that leads Bob Ewell to seek his revenge on Atticus.

Notes
exodus – general departure
Mr. Jingle – a character in Dickens' *Pickwick Papers*

CHAPTER 19

Summary
Tom Robinson is called to the witness stand to testify. He tells how he used to do small chores for Mayella Ewell. He said he helped her out because no one else ever gave her a hand. He testified that until the night in question he had never been inside the house, although he had been in the yard.

He tells how on the night in question Mayella asked him to fix a broken door hinge. When he got inside there was nothing wrong with the hinge. Mayella then asked him to take something down from the top of a chest. As he stood on a chair, Mayella grabbed him around the legs. When he jumped down, she kissed him and asked him to kiss her back. He asked her to let him by, but she refused to move from in front of the door and he didn't want to push her. It is while she was hugging him that Mr. Ewell saw them through the window and screamed at her. In the confusion Tom ran away. He swears he did not harm Mayella Ewell in any way.

The prosecuting attorney begins needling Tom, trying to make him change his story. He asks him whether Mayella is lying in her testimony and Tom says no, she is just mistaken. When the prosecutor asks Tom why he did all those chores for Mayella, Tom answers that he felt sorry for her. As soon as he has said this he realizes his mistake.

While the prosecutor questions Tom, Dill starts to cry and Scout has to take him from the court. Dill tells Scout that Mr. Gilmer's sneering cross-examination of Tom is the cause of his sickness. As he explains this to her, Mr. Dolphus Raymond, who is out of sight but able to hear the children's conversation, agrees with Dill's feeling about the trial.

Commentary

During Mayella's testimony, Scout comes to realize what a lonely person Mayella is. She has no friends or companions, no interests or schooling, and often nothing to eat. Scout also begins to understand her father, who feels sorry for Mayella even though he knows she was lying about her story. Atticus gets no pleasure out of destroying her testimony and Scout gets an inkling as to his reasons. Furthermore, Scout listens to Tom's testimony and finds herself believing his story. He seems to be a "respectable Negro." Tom's story only further emphasizes the sadness of Mayella's life. In a way, Tom was the closest thing to a friend she had and Scout realizes this.

When Mr. Gilmer begins his cross-examination of Tom, the reader gets an idea of the prejudice at work in the courtroom. Mr. Gilmer calls Tom "boy" and sneers at the answers he gives. When Mr. Gilmer gets Tom to admit that the reason he helped Mayella was because he felt sorry for her, the court is taken aback. In their eyes it is sheer effrontery for any Negro to pity a white woman. To the court audience, any white woman, no matter how poor and ignorant, is superior to a Negro. Scout and, especially, Dill realize that this is a sickening attitude.

Notes
ex cathedra – uttered with authority
buck – unpleasant slang for a male Negro

CHAPTER 20

Summary

Dill and Scout talk to Mr. Dolphus Raymond who offers Dill a drink from the bottle in his paper bag. Dill is surprised when the drink turns out to be Coca-Cola. Mr. Raymond explains that by appearing to be drunk he offers people an excuse for his outrageous behavior. He tells the children that he prefers living with Negroes but he realizes that the townspeople would never accept him if they knew the truth.

Scout and Dill return to the courtroom in time to hear part of Atticus' speech to the jury. He plainly and clearly spells out to the jury the evidence they have heard, repeating the lack of medical corroboration to Mayella's supposed rape, the beating which took place to the right side of her face and stating the reasons for Mayella's false accusation of Tom Robinson. Atticus says that in kissing a Negro, Mayella broke "a rigid and time-honored code of our society" and in an attempt to deny her guilt she accused Tom Robinson of attacking her. Atticus concludes his speech by directing the jury to remember that in the courtroom if not in life, all men are created equal.

Commentary

Through the meeting with Mr. Raymond, Scout learns a little of the power of prejudice. It is strong enough to make a grown man lie about himself and pretend to be worse than he really is. In a few minutes she will see the true power of prejudice when the jury finds Tom guilty even though everyone knows he is innocent. Mr. Raymond has told the children his secret because he knows they are young enough not to have been infected by the thinking of prejudiced adults. Their innocence allows them to see through the artificial barriers of color and to accept an individual for what he is. They do not really understand the necessity of Mr. Raymond's subterfuge but they do listen carefully while he tries to explain. Scout is beginning to learn not to accept the town's rumors as truth but the final lesson comes when she meets Boo Radley.

In his speech Atticus tries to reach the core of decency he believes to be within every man. He expands upon the idea that all men are created equal, trying to explain that this is not so anywhere but in the courtroom. As we soon see, it is not even true in court.

Notes

Thomas Jefferson – third President of the United States who drew up the draft of the Declaration of Independence

distaff side – female side

Rockefeller – philanthropist, millionaire, helped found Standard Oil Company

Einstein – physicist, author of *The Theory of Relativity*

CHAPTER 21

Summary

Calpurnia enters the courtroom to tell Atticus the children are missing. When he hears they are in the courtroom they are sent home to eat supper but told they might return to hear the verdict. Jem is confident they have won the case. He tells Reverend Sykes he doesn't see how anyone could convict Tom on the evidence they had heard. Reverend Sykes is less optimistic explaining that a jury has never decided in favor of a black man over a white man.

The jury is gone for many hours before they return with the verdict. They have found Tom Robinson guilty. As Atticus passes under the balcony on his way out of the courtroom all the Negroes rise in tribute to him.

Commentary

This is when the children see the complexity of prejudice. They had expected an easy victory based on the evidence. In their youth and innocence they had not know of the other, evil forces that would not allow a "not guilty" verdict. The jury would rather condemn an innocent black man than accept the fact that a white woman could first lust after a Negro and then lie about the fact.

For Scout there is an eerie, dream-like quality to the events. In a strange flashback she sees Atticus-the-defending-attorney like Atticus-the-slayer-of-mad-dogs. However, there is nothing unreal about the outcome of the trial. Tom Robinson has been found guilty. Atticus puts his hand on Tom's shoulder and tells him they will appeal the case in a higher court.

We have seen the little regard the townspeople have had for Atticus for taking on the case, but now we see the tremendous respect the Negroes have for him. Even though he has lost the case, they all stand and pay silent tribute to the man who so valiantly defended Tom Robinson.

Notes

exhilarated – enlivened

giving her precious Jem down the country – withdrawing protection — originates from days of the slave trade

CHAPTER 22

Summary

Jem is tremendously upset over Tom Robinson's conviction. He tells Atticus that it isn't right and Atticus agrees. The next morning Atticus tells the children he plans to appeal the case. As they make their way to the diningroom for breakfast Atticus tries to explain to Jem that this is not the first time justice has been mocked by white people.

Calpurnia shows Atticus the food that the Negroes of the town have left on his doorstep as tribute to his courage and humanitarianism. The gifts make tears come to Atticus' eyes.

After breakfast the children go over to see Miss Maudie who offers them the small comfort of her words and a generous serving of her cake. She tells Jem that Atticus is one of the men "born to do our unpleasant jobs for us." She also tries to point out to Jem the number of friends Tom Robinson has in the town, including Judge Taylor who appointed Atticus to the case. As the children leave Miss Maudie's they hear that Bob Ewell spat in Atticus' face and swore to get even with him for the humiliation he has suffered.

Commentary

Aunt Alexandra may not share all of Atticus' views but she does sympathize with her brother as we see when Atticus returns from court. She calls him "brother" and eyes him anxiously for signs of bitterness.

The white people of the town were outraged with Atticus for defending Tom Robinson and were "cheerful" over his conviction. It was the Negroes who appreciated the efforts Atticus made not just on Tom's behalf, but on the behalf of justice as well. They show their appreciation by bringing to the Finches small gifts of food, food they could probably not afford to part with. Yet they all felt it was important to demonstrate their appreciation.

Miss Maudie offers the children her wise counsel. She points out the importance of the jury's long deliberations. Usually, she tells them, a case like this would have been decided in minutes. Miss Maudie sees this as a small sign of change. She also makes them aware of the kind intentions of Judge Taylor when he appointed Atticus to the defence instead of the young, inexperienced Maxwell Green. Judge Taylor wanted Tom to have the best possible lawyer standing up for him. In a last piece of wisdom, Miss Maudie gives the children an inkling into the exceptional character of their father. Until these recent events the children had taken Atticus very much for granted. Slowly, however, they are beginning to see the unusual qualities he embodies. For Scout, her realization comes in the courtroom when she links the courage of her father facing the mad dog with the courage he demonstrates when facing a hostile court. Miss Maudie makes it clearer when she says that Atticus is the man who stands as an example to the rest of the town. He is the one who knows what it is to be a Christian.

At the end of the chapter we hear of the threat Bob Ewell makes to Atticus, a threat Atticus doesn't take very seriously but Bob Ewell does.

CHAPTER 23

Summary
Atticus tells Scout and Jem not to worry about Mr. Ewell. He explains to the children Ewell's reasons for threatening him. Atticus also explains a little of the legalities involved in the trial and how they can be wrongfully applied by a jury. Jem concludes that juries should be abolished but Atticus points out the problems this would raise. The children are surprised to learn that one of the Cunninghams, who was on the jury, wanted to acquit Tom Robinson. Scout decides to be friends with Walter Cunningham but Aunt Alexandra forbids it saying the Cunninghams are "not our kind of folks." In considering all the types of people in the world who don't get along with each other, Jem decides Boo Radley stays in the house because he doesn't want to face all the world's problems.

Commentary
Once again Atticus urges the children to stand in another's shoes in order to understand them. In this case he is trying to help them realize Bob Ewell's motivation in threatening him. However, Atticus misreads the true nature of Ewell's desires when he dismisses him as harmless. Atticus is too good to know the extent of Ewell's evil nature.

Atticus attempts to explain the reason for the trial's outcome to the children. He points out to them the weakness in the judicial system but he still feels that it is the one place where a man should be able to get a "square deal . . . be he any color of the rainbow." The problem lies in the fact that people carry their prejudices with them and are unable to put them aside when hearing a case involving a white man against a black man. Atticus tells the children that any white man who cheats a black man is trash. We soon see that Aunt Alexandra has a different notion of what trash is.

When Atticus reveals to the children that one man who held up the jury's decision was one of the Cunninghams, Scout wants to be friends with Walter Cunningham Jr. Aunt Alexandra forbids the friendship saying the Cunninghams are trash. Her definition bewilders the children who have been raised with their father's very different value system. She bases her opinion on something she calls "background." Jem thinks he understands what motivates people like Aunt Alexandra when he reasons that each class of persons despises those considered to be a lower class. Thus, Aunt Alexandra despises the Cunninghams who look down on the Ewells who in turn hate the Negroes. This thought so depresses Jem that for the first time he understands why Boo Radley remains hidden away from the world.

In reintroducing Boo's name Miss Lee prepares the reader for the episode in which Boo saves the children's lives.

Notes
circumstantial evidence – that which is not first-hand (no eye-witness to the crime)
peace bond – a court order to keep the peace
hung jury – a jury that cannot reach a unanimous decision since one (or more) member(s) declines a verdict
yap – uncouth or ignorant person
Cajuns – people of white, Indian and Negro ancestry in Southwest Alabama and sections of Mississippi
pot-liquor – thin broth

CHAPTER 24

Summary
Aunt Alexandra hosts a missionary tea and invites Scout to

join the ladies. The women have been studying the plight of a far-off tribe of natives. The conversation turns to the trial of Tom Robinson and the condition of his wife and family. During the course of the tea, Atticus returns home and tells Aunt Alexandra, Scout, Miss Maudie and Calpurnia that Tom is dead. He was shot while trying to escape from jail during exercise period. He asks Calpurnia to go with him to tell Helen Robinson. When he leaves, Scout, Miss Maudie and Aunt Alexandra return to the tea without mentioning Tom's death to the others.

Commentary

Of chief interest in this chapter is the demonstration of hypocrisy by the ladies who have attended the missionary tea. They are speaking with compassion for the neglected tribes of Africa while insulting and demeaning the Negroes who work in their homes. Scout doesn't recognize the hypocrisy for what it is, but does find that she generally prefers the company of men who do not try to insinuate their criticism behind false praise. Men, she thinks, are more forthright. Yet when Atticus comes bearing his grim news, Scout gets another picture of what being a lady entails. She sees Aunt Alexandra pull herself together and return to the tea without betraying a shadow of her upset emotions.

As a result, Scout now sees her Aunt Alexandra in a different light. She sees her as a woman capable of gratitude, one whose calm exterior can be broken momentarily. This signals the beginning of a new understanding in Scout. Not only does she better understand her aunt, she also has a notion of the qualities her aunt is trying to instil in her.

Notes

impertinence – rudeness
squalor – wretchedness
undelectable – not enjoyable
charlotte – dessert of cake and cream
yaws – contagious skin disease
Mrs. Roosevelt – wife of Franklin D. Roosevelt, President of the United States from 1933-45

CHAPTER 25

Summary

Scout lies in bed remembering what Dill had told her of the day Tom Robinson was killed. Dill and Jem were waiting for Atticus in the car while he went to tell Helen Robinson about Tom's death. Helen fainted at the news and was carried indoors. Then Scout remembers the editorial Mr. Underwood had written in his paper about the shooting. He had said it was a sin to kill a cripple and equated Tom's murder with the killing of songbirds by hunters and children. Most of the town, however, thought it was "typical of a nigger to cut and run." For the most part the town was not very interested in what happened to Tom Robinson.

Commentary

In this chapter many different images combine to reinforce the idea of Tom Robinson's innocence and the sin of his murder. Dill reports to Scout that Helen fainted when she heard the news of her husband's death. He said it was as though "a giant with a big foot just came along and stepped on her." This recalls the beginning of the chapter where Jem prevents Scout from mashing an insect. One minute man is the giant, the next instant, he himself can be felled like an insect.

In an even more obvious allusion to the title of the novel and its association with Tom Robinson, Mr. Underwood refers to Tom's death in an editorial and says it is a sin to kill a cripple just as it is a sin to kill innocent songbirds.

When Scout first reads Mr. Underwood's editorial, she cannot understand why Tom's death is referred to as a senseless killing. She reasons that since Tom had a trial and was found guilty, his death was part of the punishment. She then does understand. Tom's trial had been a lost battle from the start because the jurors' hearts and minds were closed to the truth because Tom was a Negro. In reaching this conclusion Scout has begun to lose her innocence and to see with the eyes of an adult.

Notes
lightning-bugs – fireflies
roly-poly – woodlouse

CHAPTER 26

Summary

School starts and Scout passes the Radley house on her way to and from school. The house has ceased to terrify her and she is sorry for having taken part in Boo's torment.

One day in a Current Events class the teacher tells about Hitler. She contrasts the actions in Germany with the United States and says the difference between the two countries is "democracy." Scout defines democracy as "Equal rights for all, special privileges for none." Yet Scout cannot understand how it can be alright to persecute Negroes but not anyone else. She asks Jem about this but he sends her away saying he doesn't want to hear about anything having to do with that day at court.

Commentary

Scout is maturing. The Radley place holds no terror for her and she regrets having bothered Boo in the past. As part of her maturation she now wonders about things which she had readily accepted only months before. When the teacher tries to tell the children about the difference between a democracy and a dictatorship she uses the United States as an example of the former. Scout wonders, though, how they can call themselves a democracy when they still practise prejudice against Negroes. She tries to reason it out for herself and when she cannot find the answer she asks Jem. "Isn't it as bad to persecute Negroes as it is to persecute Jews?" she asks him. Jem, however, is still unable to face the truths he has learned at the trial. He is having a difficult time realizing that people are not all good as he had formerly believed.

Notes

holy-roller – frenzied religious sect
Elmer Davis – U.S. radio commentator, analyst for Columbia Broadcasting System

CHAPTER 27

Summary

Only three slightly unusual events disturb the normal routine of that fall. First, Bob Ewell got and lost a job. He complained that Atticus had the job taken from him. Second, someone tried to break into Judge Taylor's house and, third, Helen Robinson, Tom's widow, was given a job by Tom's former employer, Link Deas. When he found out she was walking a mile out of her way to avoid the Ewell's house, he asked her about it. She answered that the Ewells taunted her and she was frightened by them. Link Deas confronted Ewell and ordered him to leave Helen alone. Things seemed to quiet down after that.

As Hallowe'en approaches we hear of the pageant the ladies of Maycomb have planned. Scout is to go dressed as a ham and appear on stage when Mrs. Merriweather calls out "pork." Her costume is constructed of chicken wire and reaches from her head down to her knees. Neither Atticus nor Aunt Alexandra are able to attend the pageant and Jem is asked to escort Scout.

Commentary

This chapter serves to create a mood of tension which prepares us for the events in the next chapter. We learn of the threatening activities of Bob Ewell and how he still remembers the humiliation he suffered at the trial. Aunt Alexandra's feeling that something will happen further heightens the atmosphere, although Scout's offhand manner can lull the reader into an expectation of calm.

Notes

National Recovery Act – Roosevelt's measure for economic recovery, part of the New Deal

Clanton – a town 90 miles north of Monroeville

CHAPTER 28

Summary

Jem and Scout make their way to the school through the darkened schoolyard. A friend of theirs, Cecil Jacobs, jumps out of the darkness and frightens them. When they reach the school Scout first goes around exploring the booths and then dons her costume and waits for her cue. While waiting, she falls asleep and misses her cue altogether. When she wakes up she goes out onto the stage, interrupting the finale.

Scout is mortified and decides not to head for home until all the people have left. She also keeps her costume on, reasoning one can hide better inside a costume. As she and Jem are crossing the dark schoolyard, Jem thinks he hears someone following them. There is a scuffle and Scout is knocked down. Jem pulls her up and shouts at her to run. Scout is knocked down again and then cannot hear Jem. When she recovers her balance and makes her way out to the road, she sees a man striding down the road with Jem in his arms. The stranger enters the Finch house still carrying Jem and Scout runs after them. Atticus calls the doctor and the sheriff. The doctor arrives first and takes care of Jem's broken arm. When the sheriff arrives he tells them that Bob Ewell is lying in the schoolyard and he is dead.

Commentary

There is a great deal of activity in this chapter. There is the scary walk the children take on their way to the school, which is later balanced by the truly frightening attack on them by Bob Ewell. Once home there is the arrival first of the doctor and then of the sheriff with his startling news. Miss Lee has allowed the events of the chapter to have a cumulative effect which is climaxed in Heck Tate's short statement "Bob Ewell's lyin on the ground under that tree down yonder with a kitchen knife stuck up under his ribs." These events are told the way Scout sees them so that for the time being the rescuer is completely ignored. Scout seems to have no idea who their mysterious savior is, although we suspect it is Boo Radley.

Notes
Poor Will – the American night-jar, a small bird whose name
    represents the sound of its call
hock – hindleg of an animal
crap games – gambling games played with two dice

CHAPTER 29

Summary
Scout recounts the events of the attack to Heck Tate and

her father. Mr. Tate points out how Scout's costume likely saved her life since the chicken wire blocked Bob Ewell's knife. He also tries to explain to Atticus the nature of Bob Ewell's evil character. When Scout reaches the part in her narrative where a man comes to rescue them, she points to the stranger leaning against the wall in Jem's room and recognizes him as Boo Radley.

Commentary

. This short chapter serves to highlight the malevolent nature of Bob Ewell and to introduce, at last, Boo Radley in person. It is here that the two themes of the novel are brought together. Bob Ewell has met his end while Arthur Radley comes to life. Arthur Radley, who had been a ghostly, horrible figure in the children's imagination, has materialized as a hero. In appearance he is as pale as the ghost or "haint" they used to fear but his shyness is immediately apparent. He is a frightened rather than frightening man.

Miss Lee ends this chapter with the startling "Hey Boo" that Scout says when she finally recognizes the stranger.

CHAPTER 30

Summary

Heck Tate and Atticus have a clashing of wills as Tate asserts that Bob Ewell fell on his own knife and Atticus insists that Jem killed him. Finally Heck Tate has to spell out to Atticus that it wasn't Jem but someone else who killed Ewell. He adds that as far as he is concerned, Ewell fell on his knife and no one else's name will be brought into the affair. When Heck leaves, Atticus turns to Scout and asks her if she understands. Scout jumps up and hugs Atticus saying Heck Tate is right. It would be like killing a mockingbird to drag Arthur Radley into the limelight. On his way back into the house Atticus stops to thank Arthur Radley for saving his children.

Commentary

In this chapter we get a firm idea of how much Scout has matured. Atticus doesn't understand what Heck Tate means when he insists that Bob Ewell fell on his own knife but Scout grasps immediately the significance of this decision. Also it is

Scout who recognizes the analogy of Boo to a mockingbird. Heck Tate has said it would be a sin to expose Arthur Radley to the limelight and Scout acknowledges that this is as much of a sin as killing an innocent songbird.

Notes
craw – stomach

CHAPTER 31

Summary
Scout understands that Mr. Arthur wants to see Jem again before heading home and so she leads him back into Jem's room. After seeing Jem, Mr. Arthur asks Scout if she will take him home. Scout lets go of his hand and takes his arm so that it appears he is escorting her down the sidewalk. When she reaches his porch and he has gone into the house, she stops for a moment and looks down the street toward her own house. She stands for a moment in his shoes and sees herself and Jem as he has seen them. She sees a little girl and a young boy playing together through all the seasons of the year. She understands that he has watched them for so long and with such love that he comes to believe that they are his children too. When they need him, he is there.

As Scout is falling asleep that night she tells Atticus that Mr. Arthur is a nice man.

Commentary
In this closing chapter, Scout has the opportunity to demonstrate the many things she has learned through the course of the novel. She is sympathetic toward Mr. Radley and his many idiosyncrasies, the lesson learned from having Walter Cunningham to lunch; she quickly realizes that to bring Mr. Radley into the limelight would be as sinful as willfully killing a mockingbird; and she experiences that moment of total empathy with another human being when she is able to see things from their point of view. Furthermore, she demonstrates her concern for Mr. Radley's dignity by refusing to lead him down the street, and she acts with a ladylike tact that would have greatly pleased her Aunt Alexandra. She has matured

greatly, from the little girl who feared the demon Boo Radley to this warm and sympathetic human being who understands Arthur Radley.

In contrast to Scout's own understanding is Atticus' mistaken judgment with respect to both Bob Ewell's threats and his murder. Perhaps it is a measure of Scout's maturity that she can see that her father does make mistakes. In any case, with Scout's acknowledgement that Mr. Arthur is really a nice person, this stage of her development is complete. The cynicism Jem had earlier felt about people hiding their evil natures under a mask of normality has given way to the optimistic sentiment that most people are really nice when you finally do see them for what they are.

Notes
raling – the sound which would come from a diseased lung

Character Sketches

Atticus Finch

Atticus Finch, Jem and Scout Finch's father, is a central figure in the novel. His high principles and strong moral attitude are put to the test when he is asked to defend a Negro accused of raping a white woman. Although the Negro is not guilty of the crime, most of the town would like to see him convicted because of their prejudice against Negroes. Atticus stands up to the townspeople and puts up a strong defence of Tom Robinson because he believes that all men should be equal in the eyes of the law. He judges all men, be they white or black, on their individual worth and not on the color of their skin.

These views are the basis for the lessons he tries to teach his children. He hopes they will not make hasty judgements about people but first try standing in their shoes in order to see things from their point of view. Perhaps it is because he follows his own instruction that he understands his children so well. His relationship with them is an important element in the novel and helps us better understand Atticus himself. The rapport he has with them leads his relatives to believe he is not bringing up his children properly. Yet in every instance we see Atticus' methods are best. When Aunt Alexandra or Uncle Jack try to teach the children a lesson in their own way, the results are never happy. Atticus treats his children with respect. He listens to their views with interest and never tries to limit the scope of their discussions. He answers their questions openly and honestly. Both children try their hardest not to disappoint him.

Atticus is the rational man in a community of emotional excesses. The townspeople may don dark clothes and hats as they form a lynch mob or may cry out loud thinking of the impoverished natives of far-off Africa, but Atticus is "the same in his house as he is on the public streets."

Just as Atticus is the voice of reason, he is also the embodiment of justice. Atticus knew before he began that there was virtually no chance of getting a "not guilty" verdict from a jury composed of Maycomb County residents. He knew the prejudices of the jury members would win over justice and Tom Robinson would be condemned. Yet he was determined to put up a good fight to ensure that everyone in the crowded courtroom understood that they were convicting an honest and inno-

53

cent man. In this way he forced them to come face to face with their own prejudices, although most of them refused to see the truth. Still, in spite of his experiences, Atticus believes in the system of justice and trial by jury. (He does admit, though, that some of the laws need changing in order to make it more difficult to convict the innocent.) It is this conviction that justice is worth fighting for that makes him representative of justice in the county.

Miss Maudie pays Atticus the highest compliments when she says, "There are some men in this world who were born to do our unpleasant jobs for us. Your father's one of them," and later adds, "We're so rarely called on to be Christians, but when we are, we've got men like Atticus to go for us." Another time she remarks, "Whether Maycomb knows it or not, we're paying the highest tribute we can pay a man. We trust him to do right. It's that simple." Miss Maudie has made it clear that it is Atticus' function to serve as an example of what is right and proper behavior. He acts as the town's moral conscience without ever preaching, chastising or condemning his fellow citizens' behavior.

Atticus is a wise, tolerant and reasonable man whether he is dealing with his children, the impoverished Negroes or the men and women who are his neighbors. He behaves with the same courtesy and respect to Mayella Ewell as to Mrs. Dubose, has the same compassion for Boo Radley as for Tom Robinson and the same understanding of Walter Cunningham as of Jem or Scout.

Jem Finch
Jem is Scout's older brother. We see him maturing through her eyes and come to realize his fine qualities as she describes his actions. He is a conscientious older brother and tries to protect Scout from the censure of Aunt Alexandra and others and from the truths he thinks she is too young to cope with.

At first Jem accepts Scout as an equal in their play, but as he grows older he treats her more and more as a youngster as he begins to come to grips with adult issues. In doing so he becomes more introspective and sensitive, finding it hard to accept people with all their frailties. Yet we can see him becoming a fine gentleman as Scout describes how he was able to soothe her injured feelings when she missed her cue in the

Hallowe'en pageant. Scout says "Jem was becoming almost as good as Atticus at making you feel right when things went wrong."

Jem was always a more placid child than Scout. As the trial approaches, Atticus tells his brother Jack that he isn't worried about Jem losing his temper, he is more concerned that Scout will insist on fighting with her fists rather than with her head. As it turns out, however, Jem does lose his temper with Mrs. Dubose and cuts off the tops of all of her camellia bushes. This episode, however, serves to teach him an important lesson about the nature of courage. As he later learns, Mrs. Dubose was breaking herself of a drug addiction so that she might face death as a free person. This realization of her courage in spite of certain defeat, later comes to bear in his assessment of Atticus and the courage his father needs to continue defending Tom Robinson in spite of the town's opposition. Jem, however, refuses to acknowledge that Tom Robinson can be found guilty and when he is convicted it is a hard blow for Jem to bear. When the decision comes down "guilty," Jem cries and shouts "it isn't fair," but after that outburst he retreats into silence to mull things over in an adult fashion. For Jem, coming to terms with adult prejudice is like coming out of the cocoon of childhood and into a world of ugliness. It takes some time before he regains his equanimity, but his innocence is lost forever.

Jem, who was always sensitive to the plight of all living things, becomes even more so after the trial. In the beginning, Jem torments Boo Radley hoping to make him appear. Yet when it comes time to build a snowman, Jem carefully removes any of the worms he comes across. When the trial is over and the verdict is known, Jem suddenly understands why Boo Radley stays in his house all the time — he's too sensitive for this world. And when Scout is about to squash a small insect he insists she leave it alone; like the mockingbird it harms no one.

Jem undergoes more of a change during the course of the novel than Scout. The years he passes through, ten to thirteen, are important ones in an adolescent's development. His change is contrasted with Scout's which is less radical. From irresponsible boy to keenly sensitive, gentlemanly Mister Jem, he is always Scout's adored older brother.

Scout
Scout is the narrator of the story and we see all the events

through her eyes. Since she is six when the novel begins and nine when it ends, her narration often has an innocent quality to it. She reports events as she sees them, often without understanding what she has witnessed.

She is, however, an intelligent, perceptive child and her observations often contain a sensitive awareness. When she is in the courtroom watching Mayella give her testimony it occurs to Scout that Mayella must be the loneliest person in the world. Then when Scout finally meets Boo Radley she realizes he would feel uncomfortable in the light and gently leads him to a chair in a dark corner of the porch. She also mentions how quickly she learns his body language. For all her sensitivity, however, she is ignorant of the warped values of most of the adults. She has inherited her father's values, and she judges individuals on their individual worth and not on the color of their skin or their social position. Thus, she wants to befriend Walter Cunningham and is interested in seeing more of Calpurnia's home life. Aunt Alexandra, acutely aware of the social position of the Finches, forbids both of these ventures.

Scout slowly comes to realize, through the course of the novel, that the values she, Atticus and Jem share are not those held by the rest of the town. For her this is a slow awakening where for Jem it comes like a thunderbolt. She argues against Jem's cynicism, saying that she believes there is only one kind of folks, just folks. She denies his perception of the class snobbery he sees all around.

Aunt Alexandra tries to teach about the value of being a member of the elite Old Families. Neither Jem nor Scout is certain what this entails although they try to work out the meaning. Even Atticus disagrees with Aunt Alexandra claiming everyone's family is as old as everyone elses. In later life Scout does realize what Aunt Alexandra had in mind but as a youngster feels she would rather spend her time in the company of men who say what they mean without being sly about it. During the course of the novel, however, Scout does come to understand her Aunt and believe there is something interesting in learning how to be a "lady."

Just as Scout comes to better appreciate her aunt, her understanding grows to include Boo Radley. At the start of the novel Scout went along with the taunting of Boo but at the end of the novel she stands on his porch and sees herself, her family and her town through his eyes. She can identify with someone else's point of view and stand outside herself to understand their perceptions. Her experiences during the course of the novel have directly contributed to this growth of her character.

Dill

Dill, or Charles Baker Harris, arrives one summer and thereafter spends his summer vacations in Maycomb. He is from Mississippi and is nearly seven years old. He becomes the special friend of Jem and Scout's "fiancé." Both Scout and Jem appreciate his ability to make up stories and invent original games. Dill particularly invents wonderful stories about his father and then, when his mother remarries, about his new step-father. We realize the true nature of his sad homelife when he runs away and tells Scout how unwanted he feels in his own home. In this way Dill's childhood is contrasted with Scout and Jem's and highlights the idyllic nature of their relationship with Atticus.

Dill's keen sensitivity makes him extremely susceptible to the harsh inequalities of the world around him. The trial of Tom Robinson, with the sneering cross-examination by the prosecuting attorney, makes him physically ill and he has to leave the courtroom. Dill tries to escape the unhappiness the world shows him by living in a world of fantasy. A world where "he had seen an elephant, and his granddaddy was Brigadier General Joe Wheeler." When the adult world intrudes on his fantasy one, in the shape of Tom Robinson's trial, Dill decides to give up on adults and become a clown because "There ain't one thing in this world I can do about folks except laugh, so I'm gonna join the circus and laugh my head off."

Calpurnia

Calpurnia is the Negro cook and housekeeper who has helped Atticus raise Scout and Jem. She has been with the family for many years and runs the household with a firm hand. Atticus tells his sister, Alexandra, that in many ways Calpurnia has been stricter with the children than a mother would have been. Calpurnia has very proper notions of behavior and does her best to see that both Scout and Jem follow them.

Calpurnia is a compassionate and understanding woman. She understands Jem's moods at the onset of adolescence and also sympathizes with Scout's feelings on first going to school. Atticus trusts her completely and speaks openly of family affairs in front of her. When Alexandra complains of this, we understand it to be a criticism of Alexandra's attitudes and not of Atticus' practice.

It is an important step in Scout's maturation to realize that Calpurnia lives in a world different from her own. Her interest is piqued by this revelation and she wants to compare lifestyles. Alexandra forbids this kind of exploration, feeling it is unbecoming for a Finch to associate with "lesser folks." Calpurnia, we understand, is a fine woman. Her morals are of a high standard and she is both loyal and proud of the Finch family. In addition, she is exceptional within the Negro community for being able to read and write although she is careful not to flaunt this. In fact, when Calpurnia attends the Negro church she modifies her speech patterns so that she sounds like the other Negroes. This action demonstrates her ability to bridge the differences between white and Negro.

Miss Maudie

Miss Maudie is one of the Finch's neighbors and, unlike the others, she is a friendly and liberal friend to the children. She genuinely enjoys the youngsters' company and bakes them cakes in appreciation of their friendship. She understands what they are feeling and is able to sympathize and offer advice without losing their respect. Scout tells us that Miss Maudie never laughs at them or gives their secrets away.

Miss Maudie is a Baptist and often at odds with the other Baptists who think her finding pleasure in life is sinful. When they quote scripture at her to prove she will end up in hell, she is able to recite alternate passages commending those who enjoy earth's bounty.

Miss Maudie is one of the few supporters of Tom Robinson and Atticus' defence of him. She refuses, however, to go to the courtroom and contribute to the "Roman carnival" atmosphere that the townspeople have created even though a man is on trial for his life. When the trial is over and the case lost, she tries to help Jem accept the outcome. She points out that a small step toward progress had been made as it took the jury many hours to come to its decision. She also makes him realize that there are more people of liberal views than he believes there are in the town.

Miss Maudie's attitudes best reflect Atticus' own, both with respect to her treatment of the children and of the town's Negroes. She despises hypocrisy and doesn't hesitate to speak out against it. When Mrs. Merriweather attempts to criticize Atticus while enjoying one of Alexandra's teas, Miss Maudie speaks out. It is as much Miss Maudie's doing as it is Aunt Alexandra's that Scout becomes intrigued with becoming a lady, for Miss Maudie knows what it is to be truly civilized. She makes the children see that Atticus also possesses this quality.

Boo Radley

Boo is an important character in the novel although he only appears in person in the last few pages. Until that time he functions more as a symbol than a character. The children imbue him with a sense of mystery and strange abilities in their early years. They see him almost as a bogeyman or fierce monster rather than as a human being. Gradually though, their opinion changes, as first Jem and later Scout come to realize he is a gentle soul. When the children find small gifts in the Radley oak tree, Jem feels that Boo must be behind them. When Jem's pants have been carefully mended he realizes that Boo must have tried to help him by fixing them. At the end of the novel when Boo saves the children's lives, even Scout realizes that he is "really nice."

Boo's actual history is somewhat unclear and most of the information the children have is based on gossip and rumor as told by Miss Stephanie. After getting into some minor trouble with the law when he was a teenager, Boo's father, mortified with the shame of the situation, locked Boo up in the house. Very little was heard of him for many years until one day Boo stabbed his father in the leg with a pair of scissors. Boo's father said no Radley was going to go to the asylum so Boo just stayed where he was under the stern eye of his father. For many years he remained unseen. When old Mr. Radley died, the town expected Boo would finally emerge. He didn't however, since his older brother, Nathan, returned home and became the replica of his dour father. Now Boo was watched over by Nathan and still locked up in the house. Gradually Boo became so accustomed to the confines of his house that he grew afraid of the outside world. His family conspired in his fear because he had shamed them. When Boo reaches out to the children it is his first contact with people from the outside world. In his limited way, Boo strongly identifies with the children and comes to see them as his particular friends. Scout realizes this when she stands on his porch and sees herself through his eyes.

Boo's compassionate love of the children leads him to do something he has not done in many years. He ventures outside and confronts another man, Bob Ewell, who was threatening the children. In this confrontation Bob Ewell is killed and the children are saved. Boo Radley, who at the beginning of the novel was a phantom and not a man, has become the hero of the story.

Tom Robinson

The second half of the novel concerns Tom Robinson and his trial. Tom has been accused of raping a white woman, Mayella Ewell. During the trial it becomes obvious he could not have committed the crime. He is a gentle and polite man who tried to befriend an ignorant and poverty-stricken white woman. He often helped her out by doing small chores for her around her shack on his way home from work. His kindness leads to his destruction because Mayella decides to try and kiss him. "She says she never kissed a grown man before an' she might as well kiss a nigger." When Mayella is caught in the act by her father, she is beaten by him and the story made to appear that she was the victim of Tom Robinson's violent attack.

Although we know that Tom didn't rape Mayella (his withered arm made it physically impossible for him to attack her), he was guilty of feeling sorry for her. In the South this is a crime of almost equal magnitude as rape. The townspeople are aghast at his presumption in pitying a white woman and so he is found guilty of a crime he didn't commit.

A guilty verdict also had to be given so that it could never be said that a white woman sexually desired a black man. If Tom Robinson had gone free, a white woman would have been guilty of breaking "a rigid and time-honored code of our society, a code so severe that whoever breaks it is hounded from our midst as unfit to live with." And so Tom Robinson is found guilty although everyone knows that he is innocent of the crime of which he was accused.

Tom Robinson is used by Miss Lee to point out the racism that was, and some would say, still is, practised in the South.

Not only are the white townspeople prejudiced against him because he is black, but even the judicial system can be manipulated against him. The Negroes may have been made equal after the Civil War but true equality, Miss Lee is saying, has not yet arrived.

Aunt Alexandra

She is a meddlesome, forceful woman, who disagrees with her brother, Atticus, for defending a Negro. According to her, Scout and Jem are allowed to run free, especially Scout, who should be taught to be a lady. She thinks that family connections ought to be uppermost in the children's minds at all times. One of her minor compensating qualities is her ability to cook and, in a time of crisis, she shows great strength of character. Not an idealist, she is fond enough of her family to stand by them in times of trouble. When she is not busy standing by them, she likes to spend her hours gossiping with women friends.

Cousin Francis

He is the cousin of Jem and Scout, who makes insulting remarks about Atticus behind his back because of the Tom Robinson case, and provokes Scout to fight with him.

Uncle Jack

He is Atticus' brother, and a doctor, who is at first angry with Scout because she swears, and furious with her when she fights with Francis. But then he comes to talk to Scout and finds out why she fought with Francis. He binds up Scout's bleeding hand and is sympathetic to her, telling her stories. He is angry with Francis, not with Scout, after learning that Scout was defending her father.

Mr. Radley

He is Boo's father, who locked his son up in the house for fifteen years, and is believed by Calpurnia to be the meanest man in town.

Nathan Radley

He is Mr. Radley's older son. After his father's death, Nathan moves home from Pensacola to take care of his brother,

Boo. Considered by his neighbors to be as mean as his father was, Nathan Radley cements up the hollow tree where Boo left presents for the children and fires a shotgun when they trespass on his property at night.

Miss Stephanie and Miss Rachel

They are eccentric, gossipy neighborhood ladies. Miss Stephanie is responsible for many fairy tales about Boo Radley, and her vicious gossip is often aimed at those who offend her sense of what is right.

Sheriff Heck Tate

He is a friend of Atticus. At the end of the book, Tate lets Boo Radley go free after he has killed Bob Ewell, father of the girl who accused a Negro of raping her.

Judge Taylor

He is an elderly, intelligent, fair-minded man who used his influence so that Atticus would get the job of defending Tom Robinson. His power is limited by the fact that the jury makes the final decision.

Reverend Sykes

He is the preacher of the Negro church who is filled with a true sense of charity and righteousness. He welcomes the Finch children to church and tries to organize his congregation to help each other out when in trouble. He attends the trial of Tom Robinson. When Atticus loses the case and walks out of the courtroom, Reverend Sykes tells Scout Finch to stand up and pay homage to her father. He says to her, "Stand up. Your father's passing."

Braxton Bragg Underwood

He is the editor, owner and printer of the town's only newspaper. Though he does not like Negroes, he finds himself supporting Atticus in his editorials both before and after the trial.

Zeebo

Calpurnia's son, he is a garbage collector and organist for

the Negro church; he was taught to read and write by his mother.

Walter Cunningham, Sr.

Father of Scout's schoolmate, Walter, Jr., he is a poor farmer from Old Sarum, in the northern part of the county, who pays off a legal debt to Atticus Finch with crops instead of cash. He is the one familiar face Scout sees among the lynch mob that comes to take Tom Robinson from jail on the night before his trial. When Scout starts a conversation with him, he and his companions disperse without violence.

Dolphus Raymond

A white man from an old Maycomb family, he is a town scandal because he lives with a Negro woman and has children by her. He is believed to be a drunkard, but on the day of the trial he reveals to the children that he really drinks only Coca Cola but keeps up a pretence of drunkenness so that his fellow townsmen can use that as an easy explanation of his way of life. His children suffer most because of his way of life — they are aliens in the world of the blacks as well as that of the whites.

Miss Caroline

The schoolteacher for the first grade, and a native of northern Alabama, she is a stranger to the eccentricities of the people in Maycomb. She has a difficult time adapting to the people and their ways.

Link Deas

The employer of Tom Robinson, he tries to stand up for Robinson during the trial. After Tom's death, Link gives Helen Robinson, Tom's widow, a job and protects her from the abusive behavior of Bob Ewell, the man indirectly responsible for the shooting of Tom Robinson.

Bob Ewell

He is a drunkard and the father of Mayella Ewell, who accuses Tom of raping and beating her. Bob Ewell does not work, lives off state welfare, and lets his family forage for itself. He is mean, ignorant and dangerous.

Mayella Ewell

So frightened is she by her father discovering her with a Negro, that she accuses the Negro of raping her. She was actually the one who invited him into the house. She is an ignorant, lonely and pathetic creature.

Mrs. Merriweather and Mrs. Farrow

They are known as the two most devout ladies in Maycomb. Scout meets them at a tea given by her Aunt Alexandra and hears Mrs. Merriweather discourse on the importance of missionary work among a far-off tribe of natives. But Mrs. Merriweather is unsympathetic to the plight of Negroes near at hand and maintains that she employs her Negro servant at $1.25 a week only as a kindness during the Depression.

Narrative Technique

There are different ways of telling the same story. If an objective, factual recitation is desired you would use a third-person narrative. In a third-person narrative there is no personal voice describing events, no character telling you what happened. If, however, you want a more personal sensation you would use a first-person narrator. This is a narrator who speaks to the reader with a sense and directness often missing in other narrative styles.

Miss Lee has chosen Scout to function as a first-person narrator in this story. Thus we immediately know that she wanted us to see the described events through Scout's eyes. This method has many strengths and some weaknesses. In order for this technique to work, we must first accept the character who is to do the reporting. It is also helpful to *like* the character as this makes us empathize with the narrator's emotions and believe the information she reports. Scout is a bright, sensitive and intelligent little girl. It is easy to sympathize with her feelings about school and to appreciate her abilities. For all her intelligence, however, she is still a child and does not always understand the full implications of the events she reports. This is sometimes amusing, as the time she thinks Miss Maudie's loud voice scares Miss Stephanie demonstrates. It is also important on a more serious level.

Scout does her best to accurately report the events concerning Tom Robinson's trial. Yet, she is unable to understand the full implication of the events. She is not certain what rape is, and she is most certainly oblivious to the social consequences of a white woman's advances on a Negro male. However, instead of being a weakness in the novel, this incongruity in the voice of the narrator and the events she is reporting adds a heightened sense of injustice. Scout's notion of justice is still untouched by a prejudiced society. It is beyond her comprehension that Tom Robinson could be convicted merely because he is a Negro. Scout's bewilderment reinforces the message Miss Lee is delivering.

Scout's narration adds two important elements to the novel and is a large factor in the novel's greatness. She contributes both humor and extra impact to the events through her naive and innocent recital. Ultimately she represents the innocence within each and everyone of us. Her incomprehension at the miscarriage of justice should be our incomprehension, her ignorance of racial prejudice should be our ignorance and her sensitivity to another's unspoken needs should be our sensitivity, too.

Style

A lot of the novel's flavor comes from the style of Miss Lee's writing. There is an innocent freshness to the words themselves, especially appropriate as the words are spoken by a child. There is also her usage of Southern speech patterns and colloquialisms, which add to our sense of a particular way of life.

Miss Lee has brilliantly adapted the language to the individual personalities of each of the different characters. Thus, Atticus' speech is different from Miss Maudie's and different again from the language used by the children. This serves not only to differentiate the speakers, but also to give us a strong sense of their character. Atticus uses legal phrases and other abstractions to illustrate the points he wants to make, while Miss Maudie's very proper grammar and word construction indicates that she is a careful, reasonable and rational person.

Scout's language is the one with which we are most familiar and it provides much of the delight of the novel. She uses simple sentence construction yet often throws in words that are surprising for one of her age. When she uses the word "morphodite" and repeats Atticus' ideas about entailments, the incongruity in her age and the ideas she expresses provides an element of humor.

Humor is very much a part of the charm of *To Kill a Mockingbird*. There are several different types of humor in the novel. There is humor in Scout's speech; as mentioned above, this is the humor found in the incongruous. There is simple, good-natured humor, found in the discussion of Dill and Scout about the origins of babies, and satire, found in some of the descriptions of the townsfolk. Also present is the cutting irony found in the trial scene, which is used to emphasize the injustice of the proceedings. All these different types of humor are found in numerous examples throughout the novel and are an important factor in the book's lasting charm and appeal.

The Road to Maturity

To Kill A Mockingbird can be read as the story of a child's growth and maturation. Almost every episode in the novel contributes something to Scout's perception of the world. Through her experiences she grows more tolerant of others, learning how to "climb into another person's skin and walk around in it." Yet this is not the only lesson she learns. Below are the key episodes and the lessons she learns from them.

Scout's first day at school: Scout first hears the often repeated lesson that to understand another person, one must try to see things from their point of view. She also learns that there are social classes in society and that poor and respectable is different from poor and ignorant.

Scout finds gifts in the tree: Although Scout may not yet realize the implications of the gifts, she later acknowledges that they must have come from Boo Radley. This is the start of her acceptance of Boo as a "nice" person.

Miss Maudie's house on fire: Boo comes to Scout's rescue by placing a blanket over her and she begins to see him as a kind man and not as a monster.

Scout fights Francis: After the fight Scout overhears her father talking and learns he wants her to fight with her head and not her fists.

Atticus shoots the mad dog: Scout learns about one form of her father's courage, his physical courage in the face of danger.

Jem destroys Mrs. Dubose's camellias: After Mrs. Dubose dies, Scout learns of her gallant fight to beat her morphine addiction. She begins to understand another form of courage.

Scout and Jem go to Cal's church: Scout realizes that Calpurnia has another life when she is not with them.

Dill runs away: Scout begins to sense her father is unlike other fathers. Her relationship with Atticus is idyllic in comparison with Dill's homelife.

Scout and the lynch mob: When Scout speaks directly to a member of the lynch mob, Walter Cunningham, without her realizing it she forces him to stand in her father's shoes, which in turn breaks up the mob. Later she realizes something of Atticus' courage in facing the mob.

The trial of Tom Robinson: Scout learns about equality and inequality, about justice and injustice and finally about racial prejudice.

Aunt Alexandra's tea for the missionary group: Scout hears the two-sided attitude of the townspeople toward African and American Negroes. This is her first encounter with hypocrisy.

Boo rescues the children from Bob Ewell: Scout finally meets Boo Radley and finds out that he is a shy but kind man. She sees herself and her brother from his point of view and comes to some understanding of him.

These are only a few of the many events in the novel that contribute to Scout's maturation and education.

The Mockingbird As Symbol

Many times during the course of the novel the idea of the mockingbird comes to mind. We first learn of the harmless bird when the children are given air rifles for Christmas. Their father warns them never to shoot the little songbird, saying to do so would be a sin. Since this is the first time that Scout has ever heard her father refer to something as a sin, she asks Miss Maudie about it. Miss Maudie explains that the mockingbird's only function in life is to make beautiful music for us to appreciate. That's why it is a sin to kill it.

Some time later, during the trial of Tom Robinson, it occurs to the reader that Tom Robinson shares many characteristics with the mockingbird. He is a gentle man who has never harmed anyone and sought only to help someone he thought was in need. His murder is as much a sin as the killing of any innocent creature, but it is even more shameful because of his gentleness.

By the end of the novel we see that Boo Radley is also like the mockingbird. He too is shy and gentle, living quietly and harming no one. When the need arises, however, he is able to save the children from the attack by Bob Ewell. When Scout is standing on the Radley porch, she realizes that Boo's action was largely instinctive and much like a threatened animal defending its young. She also is sensitive enough to realize that bringing Boo out into the limelight, which a trial would do, would be like killing a mockingbird.

Tom Robinson's persecution by the town's racially prejudiced jury and Boo Radley's persecution by the town's malevolent gossips are both likened to the killing of innocent songbirds. The mockingbird links together these two disparate parts of the novel and gives an added sense of the fragility of these two lives.

The idea of the mockingbird in connection with Tom Robinson and Boo Radley is a fairly obvious one, but the mockingbird is a symbol for other things in the novel as well. Justice, we see, is as fragile as any songbird and is sinfully "killed" by the jury who willfully ignores the evidence and finds Tom guilty of a crime he didn't commit. Even childhood itself is a fragile state as Scout, Jem and Dill demonstrate. The innocence of their lives is destroyed by the realization that the world is an often cynical and cruel place. Perhaps it is a necessary step on the road to maturity to see the cruelty in the world as well as the beauty, but it does change forever a child's outlook and "kills" his trust and confidence in adults.

The mockingbird is as much a symbol of a fragile way of life as it is an emblem of what is good and gentle in the world. Thus, in the novel the mockingbird serves to unify two distinct plot elements and add another thread to the novel's rich fabric.

Themes and Ideas

The Sympathy Theme

Through the course of the novel, Atticus repeats to Scout and Jem the necessity of seeing things from another point of view in order to understand what the other person is feeling. He is trying to instil in the children an abiding sympathy toward other human beings. Atticus is the humanitarian he is because he is able to sympathize with other people even while disagreeing with them. We see this quality in him several times during the novel, most remarkably when he sympathizes with Mayella Ewell for her sad life yet is still resolved to show how she lied in her accusation of Tom Robinson. Atticus' sympathetic nature is also evident in his attitude toward the poor farmers who threaten to lynch Tom Robinson because they are carried away by the mob and by his tremendous tolerance of Mrs. Dubose, whom he believes to be a great lady in spite of disagreeing with many of her views. Furthermore, Atticus' warm relationship with his two children is made possible by the fact that he understands them and tries to sympathize with their point of view.

Scout actively tries to follow her father's example and stand in someone else's shoes before passing judgment on them. We see her exercising her self-restraint and leaving her brother alone to work out his own problems several times in the book. Of course she is most successful when she stands on Boo Radley's porch and suddenly realizes how much she and Jem have meant to the lonely man locked up inside his house.

The Theme of Childhood

The seasons, the neighbors, the code of honor of some adults, the dishonor and eccentricities of others — everything is new to Scout. She is childhood personified, as she perceives the world, learning its way with fresh intelligence. Moreover, she startles us into the memory of our own childhood, when we played our first games and divined the rules of living with other people, appraised our classmates and overheard adults as we stood, impressionable, in dark hallways.

Scout's narration of her first lessons and her attempts to imitate her elder brother and her father remind us of the examples we chose to learn from. We feel, because of the fresh judgments she makes about the strange adult world, as if we were living again through the first sensations and impressions of a new season, or through a family crisis with the people we first admired, trusted and loved. Her special memories delight us, because they revive memories of our own childhood.

The plot of the novel is composed of remembered facts and feelings. Scout tells the story in retrospect, as she saw it happen when she was a child. While she did not always understand what she was witnessing, the events were still recorded in her memory. Her impressions of people and their actions, therefore, convey the meaning of the story. In looking back, she understands what was important, and chooses incidents which reveal their significance.

The Idealistic Hero

Scout has a special hero, her father, an idealist. Though most of his neighbors slander him, he defends an innocent Negro. Atticus has a strong sense of duty to his fellow man which he tries, by example, to teach to his children and his neighbors. He exposes and hurts another human being only when he has no other choice. He never exhibits his special gifts and knowledge, except in the service of others. A strong personality, master of himself and his children, he is the fixed value in Scout's world. Scout seeks to please him above all; she finds other people special and valuable only if they live up to the firm strictures and ethics of her father — a Southern gentleman of stature and grace.

Maturation of a Child

The story takes place over a period of years, and the reader takes part in the adventure of a child growing up in a small Southern town. Her increasing awareness of her brother as an individual, and of herself as a girl who must leave behind her tomboy ways and become a young lady, are the framework for a novel that documents that singularly Southern phenomenon — the trial of a Negro for rape.

These events teach Scout about people; she learns to accept them as they are. That she refrains from fighting with her fists at the slightest provocation, and shows compassion for the recluse, Boo Radley, whom she formerly taunted, illustrate visibly the signs of her emotional growth. Gone are the childish pantomimes on the tragedy of Boo's life, which she made up along with her brother and Dill. Time means little in itself to children. Indeed, they do not reckon life in terms of hours, days, or years, but rather in units of what they learn, and how they grow to feel about other people and how to judge their actions and experiences.

At the end of *To Kill a Mockingbird*, Scout is bewildered and saddened by how much she has learned from the violence and tragedy in Tom Robinson's story. Her brother is bitterly disillusioned by the unjust treatment accorded to Tom. Scout also learns what it means to be victims like Boo Radley and Mayella Ewell. She knows that she is fortunate in having a wonderful father who teaches her to fight ignorance and combat evildoers like Bob Ewell. Scout begins to learn that she will be responsible, as an adult, for herself and her fellow man.

While the children start maturing as individuals, they do not grow away from each other. The Finch family exists as a unit, and the people in it manage to understand, love and live in peace with one another, despite the normal alienation most people experience as they approach adulthood.

In many ways, if the story is looked upon as a song, the song is one of innocence, changed to experience.

The Theme of the Supernatural

Boo Radley is a legend, a living ghost, in the house next door to the Finch home. When, at the end of the book, he emerges as a real, lonely, pathetic creature, the superstitions about him give way to the reality of what he is.

In the same way, the dream of the South to have eternally subservient Negroes will eventually give way to the truth that Negroes and whites are equal. A few men already realize this in the 1930s. They also know that it is merely a dream to think that justice is swift and readily available to all men. Jem Finch learns that justice is sometimes impossible to achieve, when, to his lasting horror, he sees Tom Robinson denied liberty. Dreams of ghosts also come to an end for Scout and Jem. And the ghosts of the South begin to recede, as men like Atticus Finch begin to work in a real way for justice in the South of the United States of America.

The Theme of Violence

Beneath the slow and languid appearance of life in the

small Southern town, violence is always ready to erupt. The fiction of an easy alliance of white and Negro in perpetuating an ideal way of life is too often exploded by daily frictions. Atticus shoots a rabid dog, though the dog had always been friendly. In the same way, Atticus has to "pull the trigger" against Bob Ewell, who is out to destroy Negroes and any white people who want to improve the lot of Negroes. A sudden cry to justice means that a violent and unreasonable man like Bob Ewell must be stopped from wreaking havoc among temperate people.

The first evidence in the novel of how some Negroes feel toward whites is shown by the Negro woman who does not want the white Finch children in her church. She also suggests that Calpurnia is the white man's slave and mistress and, therefore, not to be respected. This hostile woman gives the first hint that the Negro has borne enough maltreatment and that some will retaliate with vehemence.

A Symbol of the Dying Past

Mrs. Dubose is an old lady who has lived all of her life in the dream world of the Southern belle, that vanished world of the South before the Civil War, where the Negroes were enslaved by a system based on the fiction of a benevolent, paternalistic power. Therefore, she cannot accept them as equals. She is an invalid wracked with pain from a long illness, exactly as the South has suffered from its policy of segregating Negroes. Mrs. Dubose takes drugs to kill the pain, but the illness cannot be cured, any more than the South can stop the Negro from being a man by denying him his rights, his humanity. He will take them anyway.

Before Mrs. Dubose dies, she gives up drugs and accepts the pain, so that she will be beholden to no one and nothing. The South, too, must struggle to take its place among the freedom-loving people of the world.

Mrs. Dubose's pride in the South is her saving grace, however. She brings her family heritage and bravery to her final battle. She sustains pain to gain her own self-respect. The South, too, is going through a painful metamorphosis to gain self-esteem. Segregation and social slavery are doomed. As Mrs. Dubose had to die, so must the sick and outdated values of the past in the South. People can no longer drug themselves with lies about Negroes. Now they are being forced to realize that

Negroes must be accepted as equals. Mrs. Dubose is a symbol of the dying order with its weapon of militant segregation and attendant backwardness.

A Symbol of the Future

Boo Radley is a man who, as a youth, was locked up in his house by his father as punishment, and isolated from friends and teachers. He is unable to be normal and grow to adulthood the way other boys do; he is damaged psychologically and, thus, unable to expiate his guilt in a normal way. In the same way, the South, after the Civil War, never really recovered from defeat. It was poverty-stricken, without proper educational and industrial facilities to help it progress with the rest of the country.

Boo Radley, however, can feel love and compassion for other people. He only needs the opportunity that his father denied him earlier. When Boo sees the two Finch children, whom he has loved from a distance, threatened, he comes out of isolation and kills the disreputable, vile man who represents the impoverished "redneck." He gives the children the right to live and prevail over people who wish to keep the South ignorant, and in shackles.

War and tradition denied the South the opportunity to develop its human resources. Led by progressive and humanitarian men who were willing to act, however, the South is emerging from the isolationism and backwardness of the past hundred years. The message is the same one that Lincoln underscored when he declared that the nation could not survive "half free and half slave."

The Theme of Decay in 20th-Century Southern Literature

To Kill a Mockingbird is the first Southern novel in modern literature that depicts Southerners hopeful about the future of their restless society, and dedicated to making the world a better place for white and black children. Most other Southern novels, notably Faulkner's, show all white people bringing about the decay of their society, or at least trying to maintain a degrading status quo. They are unwilling to learn and change.

Among the poor and the ignorant, the haters and the hated, exists a Southern liberal, Atticus Finch, who stands up for the rights of man, despite an outmoded and unfair social edict against Negroes. The edict is inhumane. Atticus has only a few supporters among the many townspeople living in accordance with an outmoded code. But he is willing to fight actively against the resistance to change which the South has erected between the races. As a Southerner and a lawyer, he declares he wants to be counted on the side of justice.

Setting

Maycomb, the quiet Southern town in which all of the action takes place, is similar in many ways to Monroeville, the Southern town where Harper Lee grew up. The trees, the weather, the description of the center of the town — all are typical of the South. There is a sense of sympathy and love for the ways of the South; it may be old, worn and even corrupt, but beauty still abounds.

Life is settled and unhurried, and there is little that can happen that will disturb the "caste system" of the families of Maycomb. Fundamentalist religious sects still flourish there, the fervor of their beliefs well nurtured in the close gossipy atmosphere where everyone knows everyone else's business.

The town's history is presented just after Aunt Alexandra comes to stay with the Finch family. A tavern was set up at the junction of two pig trails, and the town developed around that. The governor of the new county established it as an administrative capital, and Maycomb became distinguished by the fact that it had a high percentage of professionals in its population.

The elements of inbreeding and isolation turned the town into the narrow, parochial, unchanging spot which provides so ideal a setting for this drama of loneliness, stupidity and injustice.

Miss Lee also points toward the future with her subject matter. She writes of the time to come when the courts all over the country will become the great levellers and, as Atticus Finch hoped, all people equal before the law. She writes of the time when the Negro in the South will no longer have to be afraid or have to believe, "If he's white, he's right."

Apparently, the number of liberals in the South has grown, for, even in her home state, Alabama, staunchly segregationist and in turmoil over the racial question in the 1960s, critics and authorities applauded her book and honored her for it.

Humor

In contrast to the scenes of stark cruelty, racial prejudice and human isolation in the novel, is the warmth and comfort of the Finch home. The novel is prevented from depicting a totally grim picture of life in the South by the sense of joy and humor evident in the actions and observations of the children who inhabit this 'sanctuary.' Scout's child's-eye view of events allows her to perceive and relate incidents in a simple, frank and often naïvely humorous manner.

Scout's perception of the world around her can be simultaneously tragic and comic, profound and simple. When Atticus' life is threatened by the angry mob of citizens, for example, Scout's incongruous remark, "Hey Mr. Cunningham, how's your entailment getting along?" relieves the seriousness and tension of the incident. On an earlier occasion, Dill and Scout trade innocent speculations about where babies come from. Dill's theory about the source of life, though child-like and simple, comes ironically close to being an appropriate explanation of this phenomenon.

To Kill a Mockingbird offers several varieties of humor. The ironic humor in the novel depends upon the presentation of a fact or statement which has an apparent significance different from, or opposite to, its real one. The appreciation of this distinction between appearance and reality enables the reader to see the portrayal of Miss Gates as ironic. Contrasting American democracy with German politics, Miss Gates observes, "Over here we don't believe in persecuting anybody. Persecution comes from people who are prejudiced." Scout is bewildered, on a later occasion, to hear Miss Gates hypocritically remark about the presumption of Maycomb's Negro population:

I heard her say it's time someone taught 'em a lesson, they were getting' way above themselves, an' the next thing they think they can do is marry us.

There is irony in Scout's — and the reader's — recognition of the contrast between Miss Gates' words in the classroom and her candid opinions.

Scout's conversation with Mrs. Merriweather, "the most devout lady in Maycomb," gives rise to further ironic comment.

Upon questioning Mrs. Merriweather about the Mrunas, Scout is told that they are pitifully poor and immoral, and that the church ladies support the reforms and assistance being offered to these underprivileged people. Shortly afterwards however, Mrs. Farrow and Mrs. Merriweather are heard discussing the dissatisfied "darkies" and their refusal to be educated or civilized. Despite the efforts of the missionary, "there's no lady safe in her bed these nights," they decide.

Further instances of hypocrisy and irony emerge during the trial. To the townspeople, the extent of Mayella Ewell's guilt resided in her violation of the social code. "She did something that in our society is unspeakable: she kissed a black man," Atticus points out ironically. But Atticus finds Mayella guilty in the sense that she used her privileged white status to place Tom Robinson in a difficult and inescapable predicament. Tom would find himself in a compromising situation no matter how he reacted to Mayella's offer.

Also ironic is the fate of Boo Radley, the other victim in the novel. As a boy, Arthur Radley was associated with a tough group of hoodlums who were arrested for their disorderly behavior. Arthur was the only one of the boys not sent to a state industrial school, a reformatory which "was no prison and . . . no disgrace." But Arthur's strict father took a dim view of this school. Instead of receiving this relatively mild punishment, then, Arthur was given over to the care of his father, who solemnly vowed to keep his son out of future trouble. The result was that "Mr. Radley's boy was not seen again for fifteen years."

The author's vision in the novel is often satiric as well as ironic. Satire takes a critical and usually humorous look at the shortcomings of human institutions. The satirist attempts to make his audience recognize the absurdities of man and the frailties of his institutions and, through laughter, inspire reform of these shortcomings.

One of the targets of Harper Lee's satire is the educational system. The misguided teaching methods of Miss Caroline, rather than Miss Caroline herself, are clearly satirized. Although Scout already knows how to read, and has known for some time, Miss Caroline, unable to cope with her pupil's advance level of learning, tells Scout:

Now you tell your father not to teach you any more.
It's best to begin reading with a fresh mind. You tell
him I'll take over from here and try to undo the
damage . . . .

Miss Caroline's response to Scout's reading ability indicates
that the system is too rigid to adapt to individual needs or local
conditions. It is a lack of consideration for local conditions that
is evident in the teaching of current events to third grade classes:

The idea was profound, but as usual in Maycomb it
didn't work very well. In the first place, few rural
children had access to newspapers, so the burden of
current events was born by the town children, con-
vincing the bus children more deeply the town children
got all the attention anyway.

The different forms of humor in the novel arouse different
responses. The spontaneous, simple humor of the children
expresses both their innocence and their profound, although
inadvertent, wisdom. The irony in the novel illustrates the hypocrisy and lack of sensitivity on the part of certain characters,
while the satire against the educational system emphasizes the
contrast between narrow-minded, formal schooling in
Maycomb and the liberal education received by Scout and Jem
from Atticus.

*The Credibility of Harper Lee's Southern Vision

To Kill a Mockingbird is a simple and likable novel about the South which occasionally reminds us of profounder, more troubling works that came before it. We do not read about the children in Harper Lee's book without remembering a famous story of William Faulkner's, "That Evening Sun," in which the innocent prattle of the three Compson children serves as an ironic counterpoint to the terror of their Negro servant Nancy; when we read about Miss Lee's Maycomb, we remember the picture of a dusty Southern town during the Depression in Carson McCullers' *The Heart is a Lonely Hunter.*

This is not to say that Harper Lee has necessarily been influenced by either of these writers. Perhaps she only shares with them the experience of a Southern childhood. Harper Lee writes a clear, unpretentious prose which shows no influence of either the best or worst of Faulkner's rhetorical style. Her Scout Finch may remind us of Carson McCullers' motherless tomboys — Mick Kelly in her first novel, Frankie Addams in *The Member of the Wedding* — but Harper Lee is uninfluenced by Mrs. McCullers' vision of loneliness as the sealed and inescapable fate of her characters.

But *we* are influenced by them, and if we have read Faulkner and Carson McCullers first, Harper Lee's sunnier picture of Southern life is apt to carry less conviction than theirs. In one of his letters to his daughter, F. Scott Fitzgerald replied to a question from her about originality in art by quoting a remark of Picasso's: "You do something first and then somebody else comes along and does it pretty." *To Kill a Mockingbird* is a pretty book in that sense.

The novel invites us into a small Southern town where everybody knows everybody else, and just as we willingly enter Grovers Corners, New Hampshire, in Thornton Wilder's *Our Town* or the Missouri town of Tom Sawyer's boyhood, we feel a nostalgia for Harper Lee's Maycomb even if we happened to grow up in a very different kind of place.

As the story unfolds we are quietly and unobtrusively told a good deal about the town's history and topography, and about the social structure of its citizenry. Maycomb is a county seat,

*By Walter Clemons, 1965.

82

with a large proportion of professional people. It is a Methodist and Baptist community, with one Jew, the storekeeper Levy, and no Catholics. Scout Finch belongs to one of the old families of the county; the Finches have "background" but no money, thereby differing from the landowning Raymonds, the "cotton-buying" but in fact idle Radleys, and the dying Mrs. Dubose, all of whom seem to have financial means of one sort or another. Atticus Finch's law practice brings him and his children into broad contact with all elements of the community, from the small farmers like Walter Cunningham who are harder hit than the Finches by the Depression, to the poor whites represented by Bob Ewell, the one character in the book without a redeeming trait. Through her visit to Calpurnia's church in Chapter Twelve, Scout is plausibly enabled to see into the Negro community, with its own differences in education and divisions of opinion.

This sense of a whole community, with its gossip and its local customs and peculiarities, is one of the "old fashioned" pleasures of reading nineteenth-century novels, and its presence here is one of the most appealing qualities of Harper Lee's book. It is supported by a wealth of remembered detail:

> Somehow, it was hotter then: a black dog suffered on a summer day; bony mules hitched to Hoover carts flicked flies in the sweltering shade of the live oaks in the square. Men's stiff collars wilted by nine in the morning. Ladies bathed before noon, after their three-o'clock naps, and by nightfall were like soft teacakes with frostings of sweat and sweet talcum.

Some reviewers of the book expressed doubts about the credibility of Scout's wide knowledge of the life in her town, but for the most part it is believable. A six-year-old Southern child who kept her ears open could easily acquire, from the leisurely gossip of her elders, the body of anecdotal information that Scout is able to provide. The courtroom scenes are the severest strain on credulity; the very presence of an eight-year-old Southern girl at a rape trial is an implausibility we grant to the author in her need to get her story told, but she goes a little too far in granting Scout the ability to recognize the pattern in her father's cross-examination of Mayella Ewell which eludes the prosecuting attorney Mr. Gilmer. Scout's knowledge of legal tactics is the knowledge of Harper Lee the law student.

But through Scout Finch, Harper Lee gives us a quantity of fascinating Southern lore, some of it startling, like the information that Calpurnia prepared Scout's patent leather shoes for church by polishing them with a cold biscuit until she saw her face in them. We trust Harper Lee in every detail of the daily life of Maycomb.

Where we trust her less is in the accumulation of incidents in her story which go to show that "Most people are [real nice] . . . when you finally see them." No single incident in *To Kill a Mockingbird* is impossible to credit, but as one event after another illustrates this dictum, it is hard not to feel that life is being prettified.

We can believe in Boo Radley. Here Miss Lee has over-turned one of the staple properties of Southern fiction, the closed house whose walls conceal a terrrible secret from the light of day. When Scout asks if Boo is crazy, Miss Maudie Atkinson's answer conjures up in our imaginations the haunted mansions in Southern literature, from Edgar Allen Poe down to Faulkner's "A Rose for Emily":

> If he's not he should be by now. The things that
> happen to people we never really know. What happens
> in houses behind closed doors, what secrets —

But when the recluse emerges, he proves to be a kindly soul who saves the lives of Scout and Jem: a representative of the guilt-ridden Old Southern aristocracy emerges from shadowy seclusion to fight for the future which the children represent. Mrs. Dubose, in a less positive way than Boo Radley, points the same moral; at the end of her life she summons her strength to free herself from the drug that offered her a refuge from pain.

We can accept these two characters. It is harder to believe in the lynch mob that is deflected from its purpose and dispersed by the opportune arrival and a few well-chosen words from an eight-year-old girl, a scene unsurpassed since Shirley Temple put down an Indian uprising in *Wee Willie Winkie*. But we may grant the possibility, and grant Miss Lee even the detail of Tom Robinson's withered left arm, which so drastically simplifies the issue of Tom's innocence at the trial. A braver writer might have risked real doubt and complexity here, by making Tom a man who *could* have committed the crime he is tried for. But then this would have introduced a complication in the character of Bob

Ewell, who might have been a less simple villain, confused and convinced of the truth of his accusation. Harper Lee presents a simplified trial of pure right versus sheer wrong, avoiding a deeper consideration of the tragic tangle of truth and falsehood which such a case might involve.

But there finally comes a point when the reader rebels at these simplifications of life. For me it comes in a scene which could have been omitted without disturbance to the story line, and that is when Dill retires from the courtroom with Scout and is offered a sip from the camouflaged bottle of Dolphus Raymond, the notorious town drunkard who lives with a Negro woman. Raymond reveals to the children that his Coke bottle which is supposed to contain whiskey contains only Coca Cola, and that when he comes into town and staggers on Main Street, he does so only to provide the citizens of Maycomb with an easy explanation of his way of life. Now there may indeed exist such saintly pretenders; Harper Lee may once have known just such a man in Alabama. I confess I cannot swallow it, and I wish she had spared us Dolphus Raymond. He does go to show, once more, that people are "real nice" when you get to know them, but Harper Lee might have chosen a harder example and have better convinced us.

Horton Foote's *The Screenplay of "To Kill a Mockingbird"* (Harvest Book, Harcourt, Brace & World, Inc.) won the Academy Award in 1964. It is a model of sensitive and tactful adaptation, and deserves study by anyone interested in the problems of dramatizing a story effectively. It opens with an incident mentioned but not directly presented in the novel, the delivery by Walter Cunningham, Sr., of a sack of hickory nuts in payment of his debt to Atticus; Scout meets him in the yard and calls her father out of the house to thank him, which embarrasses Cunningham. After a brief conversation with Atticus about the Depression, reproduced from the novel, Scout and Jem are called to breakfast by Calpurnia. But Jem will not come: he is up in the tree house, refusing to descend unless Atticus will agree to play football for the Methodists.

The first incident, Mr. Cunningham's visit, strengthens our belief in the important scene much later in front of the jail; we are better prepared for what happens there by having seen both Scout and Atticus face to face with Walter Cunningham here. The next episode, with Jem's complaint about Atticus, "Every time I want him to do something . . . he's too old . . . . He's too old for anything," relieves another important scene, Atticus' shooting the mad dog, from the slight taint of patness it has in the novel. Jem's dissatisfaction with his father is mentioned for the first time at the opening of Chapter Ten and immediately thereafter "solved" by Atticus' performance with the shotgun. Horton Foote has changed very little; but by rearranging some elements in the story, and eliminating others, he was able to bring out the best qualities of the book. The screenplay refutes the common belief that film adaptations tend to vulgarize the original material; here the screenwriter has removed some extravagances from the story, of which one small example may be mentioned: when Jem goes back to the Radley collard patch for his lost trousers, in the screenplay he simply finds them folded over the fence, without the added embellishment, in the novel, of Boo Radley having stitched them up.

In transferring the story to the screen, however, it was not necessary to alter or improve the strongest element of the book. Atticus Finch is a solidly created and entirely believable good man. With the possible exception of the incident with the mad dog, Miss Lee's portrayal of him is free of contrivance. Instead of feeling forced to invent episodes that exhibit or prove his worth, she simply puts him before us, and he convinces us. Here she has outdone William Faulkner, whose Southern lawyer Gavin Stevens is an unendurable windbag by comparison.

Miss Maudie Atkinson's testimony that "Atticus Finch is the same in his house as he is on the public streets" is one definition of his honesty. In his house and in the street, he always tries to tell the truth: when Scout asks him what rape is, she is unhesitatingly given the blunt legal definition of the crime. On another occasion, Atticus is rebuked by his sister for saying in front of Calpurnia that Braxton Underwood despises Negroes; Alexandra's reason is an interesting one: not that Calpurnia's feelings may be hurt, but that such frankness "encourages them."

The vexed Southern subject of "background" is a bone of contention between Atticus and his sister. He is enough a product of his own background to be swayed, temporarily, by Alexandra's notions on how children should be brought up; but after a brave stab at giving them a lecture according to Alexandra's lights on the matter, he gives up and becomes himself again. Atticus believes, like his sister, that the people of Maycomb County are divisible into two groups, those with "background" and those who are trash, but they disagree on the qualifications for inclusion. Unlike Alexandra, Atticus believes that the categories are not fixed, and that the white man's treatment of the Negro is a test of his quality. He tells Jem:

> As you grow older, you'll see white men cheat black men every day of your life, but let me tell you something and don't you forget it — whenever a white man does that to a black man, no matter who he is, how rich he is, or how fine a family he comes from, that white man is trash.

This belief brings him into conflict not only with easily identifiable trash like Bob Ewell, but with members of his own class who are able to despise Ewell while allowing his point of view to prevail in cases like that of Tom Robinson. The aristocratic Mrs. Dubose uses Bob Ewell's word for Atticus: he is a "nigger lover." Atticus calmly accepts the charge.

> "Scout," said Atticus, "nigger-lover is just one of those terms that don't mean anything — like snot-nose. It's hard to explain — ignorant, trashy people use it when they think somebody's favoring Negroes over and above themselves. It's slipped into usage with some people like ourselves, when they want a common, ugly term to label somebody."
>
> "You aren't really a nigger-lover, then, are you?"
> "I certainly am. I do my best to love everybody . . . I'm hard put, sometimes — baby, it's never an insult to be called what somebody thinks is a bad name. It just shows you how poor that person is, it doesn't hurt you . . ."

The final word on Atticus' relation to "background" is delivered by Miss Maudie Atkinson, according to whom Atticus is not as alone as he appears to be.

> ". . . have you ever thought of it this way, Alexandra? Whether Maycomb knows it or not, we're paying the highest tribute we can pay a man. We trust him to do right. It's that simple."

"Who?" Aunt Alexandra never knew she was echoing her twelve-year-old nephew.

"The handful of people in this town who say that fair play is not marked White Only; the handful of people who say a fair trial is for everybody, not just us; the handful of people with enough humility to think, when they look at a Negro, there but for the Lord's kindness am I." Miss Maudie's old crispness was returning: "The handful of people in this town with background, that's who they are."

It will be noticed that both the quotations above contain a strong element of sermonizing. Harper Lee is a writer with a message, but her handling of the character of Atticus is such that his attitudes, the things he stands for, never swamp his humanity or make him intolerable. His fatigue, his vulnerability, his quiet humor are as believable as his nobility. I have complained that Miss Lee sometimes fails to convince us, but her book is solid at its center. The creation of Atticus Finch was a considerable accomplishment, and the popular success of *To Kill a Mockingbird* was a deserved one.

Selected Criticisms

This Pulitzer Prize-winning novel was greeted with a great deal of critical excitement when it was first published in 1960. Harper Lee was compared to other well-known contemporary Southern writers, such as Carson McCullers, Eudora Welty and Truman Capote. Capote, himself, said that Miss Lee was "a writer with the liveliest sense of life and the warmest, most authentic humor."

In December, 1960, the critic, Leo Ward, wrote in *The Commonweal*:

> Both the style and the story seem simple, but no doubt it is quite an achievement to bring them to that happy condition. What a greenhorn from the North may enjoy most is how quietly and completely he is introduced to ways of seeing, feeling and acting in the Deep South.

A book reviewer for the *New York Times Book Review,* tempered the praise with the following criticism:

> The praise that Miss Lee deserves must be qualified somewhat by noting that oftentimes Scout's expository style has a processed, homogenized, impersonal flatness quite out of keeping with the narrator's gay, impulsive approach to life in youth. Also, some of the scenes suggest that Miss Lee is cocking at least one eye toward Hollywood. Moviegoing readers will be able to cast most of the roles very quickly, but it is not disparagement of Miss Lee's winning book to say that it could be the basis of an excellent movie.

Don Uhrbrock, writing for *Life Magazine,* was whole-hearted in his admiration, however:

> ... Miss Lee writes with a rare compassion that makes her novel soar. To me, it is the best contemporary novel I have read since 1939.

Many critics admired the style and humor of the work, though they found that the deeper seriousness of the central theme was at times at variance with the easy graciousness of style. In the July 10, 1960 issue of the *New York Herald Tribune Book Review*, Harding Lemay made this complaint:

In her first novel, *To Kill a Mockingbird*, Miss Harper makes a valiant attempt to combine two dominant themes of contemporary Southern fiction — the recollection of childhood among village eccentrics and the spirit-corroding shame of the civilized white Southerner in the treatment of the Negro. If her attempt fails to produce a novel of stature, or even of original insight, it does provide an exercise in easy, graceful writing and some genuinely moving and mildly humorous excursions into the transient world of childhood.

The two themes Miss Lee interweaves throughout the novel emerge as enemies of each other. The charm and wistful humor of the childhood recollections do not foreshadow the deeper, harsher note which pervades the later pages of the book. The Negro, the poor white girl who victimizes him, and the wretched community spirit that defeats him, never rise in definition to match the eccentric, vagrant, and appealing characters with which the story opens. The two worlds remain solitary in spite of Miss Lee's grace of writing and honorable decency of intent.

Such were the reactions of her contemporaries. It remains for time to prove the worth of this novel in the wide field of literature.

Review Questions and Answers

Question 1.

Show how *To Kill a Mockingbird* is related to its historical background.

Answer

The novel is set in the early 1930's, during the Great Depression. In the United States and elsewhere, this time was marked by radical social and political changes, some of which are evident in the novel.

The Depression had a devastating effect on the small farmer. Situated in an agricultural area, the town of Maycomb would rely heavily on the farmers, whose produce would both supply the town and provide personal income. Families such as the Cunninghams lost their sole source of income when they were unable to sell their crops. Consequently, crops went to ruin and the farmers were forced to abandon their land and seek employment in the cities. This is the unwelcome prospect that the Cunninghams face when they are no longer able to farm.

The novel contains several more direct references to social movements and political events of the times. The author occasionally calls our attention to what is taking place in Washington in the Roosevelt administration. Programs were being instituted by the government to revive economic stability and promote prosperity. The country was undergoing massive changes while rural towns such as Maycomb remained helplessly fixed in their worn traditions.

Question 2.

In what way is *To Kill a Mockingbird* typical of Southern literature in the twentieth century?

Answer

The notion of a decaying world enters into many of the novels of William Faulkner, perhaps the foremost Southern writer of this century. The plays of Tennessee Williams contain an undercurrent of change that also threatens to destroy the lifestyles and cherished illusions of many of his characters. The unwillingness to grow and change with the times is a recurrent failing in the characters portrayed in Southern literature.

The indifference or inability to adapt to change also appears in *To Kill a Mockingbird*. The static and uncompromising attitudes of the townspeople must eventually give way to newer and more humane attitudes. Atticus Finch emerges as the champion of a more liberal moral code. Although he has only a few supporters for his radical cause, Atticus fights a strong battle against an unjust and outdated social edict against Negroes.

To Kill a Mockingbird is unique in that it is perhaps the first modern Southern novel to end on a hopeful note. Although Tom Robinson is found guilty, Atticus' weighty closing remarks to the jury (and to the reader) suggest that a better future awaits coming generations.

Question 3.

In what sense is *To Kill a Mockingbird* a realistic novel?

Answer

The novel can be considered realistic because it truthfully records events as they were at that time in the South. There is no attempt on the part of the author to rationalize or idealize any of her childhood recollections. Instead, she relates situations — both pleasant and unpleasant — as they then existed. People were prejudiced and insensitive to the suffering of others, and injustice often triumphed over justice.

Harper Lee's realism does not merely include an uncompromising picture of evil, though. Reasonable people are also presented in the novel, although there are comparatively few of them. Atticus represents justice in the novel, and his active opposition to the attitudes and actions of most of the townspeople adds to the realism of the story.

Other details which add to the realistic presentation of people and events in the book are the author's ability to capture the nuances of Southern speech and convey the attitudes prevalent in a town such as Maycomb. These realistic touches are not marred by any obvious statements of the author's personal viewpoint. The author merely records events in faithful detail without making outright judgments.

Question 4.

In what way does Atticus Finch represent the novel's center of interest?

Answer

Atticus occupies a crucial position in the novel since he embodies its theme: the struggle for human understanding in the form of justice and tolerance. Atticus' point of view represents the balanced, reasonable outlook toward which other characters should ideally strive. Throughout the novel, Scout and Jem contrast the moral integrity and essential goodness of their father with the hypocrisy and evil that surrounds him. Atticus thus emerges as a model of virtue and humanity. He represents the conscience of the town, the wise tutor and parent of his children and the chief protagonist of the novel.

Question 5.

Describe Jem's function and importance in the novel.

Answer

Although Jem is not as central a figure as Scout, the narrator, his function is to reflect the mood and theme of the novel. In the course of the story, Jem develops, both physically and mentally, from boyhood to young manhood. Jem's maturation subtly parallels the changes taking place in the South. By tracing Jem's progress, then, we can also detect signs of developing Southern attitudes toward the central issue of racial prejudice.

When we meet Jem at the beginning of the novel, he is spirited and carefree. During the second section of the novel, both Jem and the story itself undergo a profound change. As the Tom Robinson story is developed, Jem becomes a more serious and moody character who carefully observes the trial. His confidence that Tom will be acquitted and, later, his bitter disappointment at Tom's unfair conviction, reveal the extent of Jem's involvement in this issue. Jem also becomes the victim of Bob Ewell's attack on the children, and he suffers a broken arm from which he will never completely recover. What happens to Jem is, in a sense, symbolic of what happens to the South in its dawning awareness of inhumanity and injustice. Jem represents the Southerner who develops a social conscience, who learns to disapprove of the actions and attitudes of his fellows, and who is permanently scarred in his attempt to overcome existing prejudices.

Question 6.
What does Dill contribute to the novel?

Answer
Dill represents the point of view of the outsider in the novel. Dill is not from Maycomb. Therefore, he is an observer of events more than a participant in them. His function in the story, in other words, is to provide a picture of how a stranger would react to the situation. Dill's distress at the outcome of the trial is therefore representative of the outsider's shock and indignation at the treatment of the Negro in the South.

Dill's role in the novel is not totally passive, though. He also affects the action of the story. His imagination and sense of adventure influence Scout and Jem. If not for Dill's overriding curiosity, the other children would not dare to invade Boo Radley's privacy as they do in their attempt to catch a glimpse of this mysterious figure.

Question 7.
Account for Aunt Alexandra's preoccupation with family and tradition.

Answer
Aunt Alexandra's concern for her family and heritage is a trait typical of many Southerners who, since Civil War times, became victims of genteel poverty. The 'old guard' Southerners prized their memories of vanished wealth and power. Atticus explains that Aunt Alexandra, having lost her family fortune, could take pride in nothing but family honor. Her husband, whose chief interest had been fishing, was unable to provide her with either security or position. Atticus and Jack had found new identities in their careers. Atticus had become a successful lawyer and had the additional responsibility of raising his two children, and Jack had found fulfillment in medicine. But Aunt Alexandra, rather than developing in new directions, preferred to dwell in the past.

Question 8.
Identify the hero of the novel and explain the reasons for your choice.

Answer
The hero of the novel, both for the reader and for Scout, the narrator, is Atticus. Despite the insults hurled at him by the

outraged townspeople, Atticus is driven by conscience to defend Tom Robinson, a Negro. Atticus reveals a strong sense of responsibility to and respect for the rights of his fellow man, and these are qualities he attempts to instil, by example, in his children and the people of Maycomb. To Scout, he represents the measure of all virtue and truth. She judges other people in terms of Atticus' firm ethical standards and attributes. To Scout and the reader, then, he emerges as a pillar of justice and a model of dignity.

Question 9.

Discuss how violence operates as a thematic concern in the novel.

Answer

Maycomb appears to be a quiet and contented little Southern town, but beneath this peaceful surface is a powerful undercurrent of violence. The harmony that seems to exist between white and Negro in this town is disrupted daily by minor outbursts of friction. The Tom Robinson trial allows us to witness a major explosion of racial hostility.

At one point in the novel (Chapter 10), Atticus shoots a once-friendly dog that has become rabid. Similarly, Atticus must take an offensive position against Bob Ewell, who threatens to destroy the Negro population and its white sympathizers.

Racial hostility in the novel is not merely one-way, as we realize when one Negro woman voices a menacing complaint against the Finch children when they enter the Negro chapel with Calpurnia. Friction between members of the same race is also aroused during this incident, for this same woman also suggests that Calpurnia's loyalties are suspect because she is the servant of a white family. These bitter words indicate the resentment with which the Negro population regards the oppressive white community. Such maltreatment as the Negroes have endured is certain to lead to retaliation through reverse discrimination.

Question 10.

How is the theme of appearance and reality developed in the novel?

Answer

At the beginning of the novel, Boo Radley is a mystery, a living ghost who 'haunts' the house next door. Although Scout,

Jem and Dill weave an exotic fantasy about their unseen neighbor, Boo Radley emerges at the end of the book as a very real and lonely person. The superstitions surrounding him are thus dispelled by the children's ultimate realization of his reality.

The theme of appearance and reality also works its way into the main issue of the novel: racial conflicts in the South. The eternal enslavement of the Negro population is an unjust and impracticable notion to which the whites stubbornly cling. Such unequal distribution of power is a dream that must eventually give way to the truth of civil equality. In the 1930's, this truth was just beginning to receive more widespread recognition in the South. Several characters in the novel, through witnessing the trial of Tom Robinson, come to realize that swift and impartial justice is an illusion. The novel illustrates that injustice is often a harsh reality.

Suggested Study Topics

1. Describe the different kinds of courage brought out in the novel.
2. In what ways is Miss Maudie like Atticus?
3. Discuss the strengths and weaknesses of using Scout as a narrator. How would the novel differ if an objective, third-person narrator had been employed?
4. What function does Dill serve?
5. What is Aunt Alexandra's effect on Scout? On Atticus? How and why does Scout's perception of her change?
6. What do you think makes the Finches different from the Cunninghams and the Cunninghams different from the Ewells?
7. "Background doesn't mean Old Family, . . . I think it's how long your family's been reading and writing." Discuss.
8. The Civil War is one of the most popular subjects for writers in the United States. There are thousands of fiction and nonfiction books on the slave trade, the abolitionists, the war itself and the government in the South directly after the war. For example, Winston Churchill's book, *The Crisis*, deals with abolitionists, people who were against slavery throughout the country. Does the nineteenth-century man's feelings about slavery, as represented in this book, differ substantially from those espoused by Southern writers today? Choose from any of the works of William Faulkner for comparison.
9. In South Carolina, directly after the Civil War, Negroes held all public offices in Columbia. Examine the role they played in the postwar South and discuss the effectiveness of their legislative programs.
10. George Washington Carver is a Negro who endured hardship to become a great scientist. A brilliant man, he succeeded despite the fact that the training so necessary for his work was almost impossible to attain. Books about this brilliant scientist are available in all libraries. Compare the hardships he endured with those of Booker T. Washington. Have things improved since then?
11. Spirituals and jazz, for which America is famous, were born in the South and nurtured by Negroes who caught a certain spirit of the country in music. Biographies of both

Billie Holiday and Louis Armstrong have been published. Compare and contrast their careers and the influence they have had on American life.

12. Negro writers, notably James Baldwin, who wrote *Go Tell It on the Mountain* and *Nobody Knows My Name*, illuminate the special problems the Negro has faced in America to find recognition and self-respect. The problems are complex. Compare and contrast the different methods he employs when he uses nonfiction rather than fiction to write about these major themes and problems.

13. A short story by Ivan Gold, in a collection of short stories called *Nickel Miseries*, brilliantly illustrates the plight of a Negro like Tom Robinson in the modern U.S. Army. The story is called "The Nickel Misery of George Washington Carver Brown." Compare the hero of this story with Tom Robinson.

14. Study the recent civil rights laws and discuss whether Tom Robinson's problem could have occurred at the present time.

15. Touissaint L'Ouverture was the leader of the slaves in the nineteenth-century uprising in Haiti. The progress made by freed slaves in Haiti and Negroes in America can be compared and analyzed, so that the student can judge how far the United States has gone in bettering the condition of all its citizens.

16. Discuss whether Shakespeare's *Othello* is the tragedy of a man who has suffered from racial prejudice.

17. Truman Capote, Carson McCullers, Flannery O'Connor and Eudora Welty are four contemporaries of Harper Lee. Select one of these major writers and compare his or her view of life in the South today, and the attitudes of the races toward each other with those of Harper Lee.

Bibliography

Adams, Phoebe. "Summer Reading," *Atlantic Monthly* (New York), CCVI, 98.

"A Review," *Booklist* (Chicago: American Library Association) LVII (September 1, 1960), 23.

"A Review," *Bookmark* (New York), XIX (July, 1960), 261.

"A Review," *Commonweal* (New York), LXXIII (December 9, 1960), 289.

"A Review," *Library Journal* (New York: R. R. Bowker), LXXXV (May 15, 1960), 1937.

"Briefly Noted," *New Yorker,* XXXVI (September 10, 1960), 203.

"A Review," *Time* (New York), LXXVI (August 1, 1960), 70.

"A Review," *Times Literary Supplement* (London), 697.

Dave, R.A. *"To Kill a Mockingbird*: Harper Lee's Tragic Vision," *Indian Studies in American Fiction,* eds. Naik, Desai and Mokaski. Pinekar, Delhi, 1974.

Erisman, Fred. "The Romantic Regionalism of Harper Lee," *Alabama Review* (1973).

Ford, Nick A. "A Battle of the Books: A Critical Survey of Significant Books by and About Negroes Published in 1960," *Phylon,* XXII.

Hicks, Granville. "Three at the Outset," *Saturday Review of Literature* (New York) XLIII (July 23, 1960), 15.

Iles, Francis. "A Review," *The Guardian* (New York), XIII (December 9, 1960), 7.

Lemay, Harding. "Children Play; Adults Betray," New York *Herald Tribune* (July 10, 1960), 5.

Lyell, F.H. "One Taxi Town," New York *Sunday Times* (July 10, 1960), 5.

McDonald, W.U., Jr. "Harper Lee's College Writings," *American Notes and Queries* (New Haven, Conn.), 6: 131-32.

McMichael, George. "A Review," San Francisco *Chronicle* (July 31, 1960), 23.

Moritz, Charles. editor, *Contemporary Biography Yearbook*. New York, 1961.

Sullivan, Richard. "A Review," Chicago Sunday *Tribune,* XIX (July 17, 1960), 1.

Uhrbrock, Don. "Literary Laurels for a Novice," *Life Magazine,* May 26, 1961.

NOTES

NOTES

NOTES

NOTES

NOTES